The Forgotten Shores

*Stories of the Wirral coast from Eastham Ferry
to Magazine Brow*

by

Maurice Hope

*COVER DESIGN:
ERIC MONKS*

To the Memory of
my Mother.

First published 1988 by Countyvise Limited, 1 & 3 Grove Road, Rock
Ferry, Birkenhead, Wirral, Merseyside L42 3XS.

Copyright © Maurice Hope, 1988.

Photoset and printed by Birkenhead Press Limited, 1 & 3 Grove Road,
Rock Ferry, Birkenhead, Merseyside L42 3XS.

ISBN 0 907768 03 2

ACKNOWLEDGEMENTS

A series of articles which appeared in 'Cheshire Life' from 1976 to 1982 formed the basis for 'The Forgotten Shores'. I am very grateful to the editor of 'Cheshire Life', Priscilla Hodgson, for allowing me to retain some of the titles of, and several passages from the original articles.

I am particularly indebted to the Chairman and Committee of the Birkenhead History Society who have allowed me to use a number of extracts from the Newsletter, and to some individual members of the Society who have given me both constant encouragement and much interesting and original material. Indeed I have borrowed recollections from numerous local residents including Bessie Cockburn, Caroline Green, Jean Hocking, Dorothy Harden, A.H. Jones, E. Lavell, F. Hoblyn, H. Foster, R.E. Roberts, J. Ashton, J.W. Gray and my mother, Phyllis Hope. I am most grateful to all of them for their contributions to the text.

I have also called upon the works of local writers who over the years have published their impressions in various books and journals. These include W.F. Bushell, G.W. Parkin, A. Watson, W.R.S. McIntyre, H.H.G. Arthur, R. Stewart Brown, P. Sulley, J.E. Allison, B. Furniss and I. Roth.

Finally, I must thank Alison Groves for original photographs and Pamela Jordan who has converted my untidy scribble into a clear and accurate manuscript.

CONTENTS

INTRODUCTION

From the entrance of the Manchester Ship Canal near Eastham Ferry to the northern boundary of Birkenhead docks industrial man has left an indelible mark. The land, the air and the water are overwhelmed by his occupation. On the low once-wooded plateau beside the River Mersey, factories and high walls, impounded docks, warehouses and acres of storage tanks testify to his energy, while the strident sounds and bitter smells of the atmosphere and the polluted waters of the estuary underline his carelessness.

The land is crowded with industrial shapes. Hissing pipelines criss-cross the countryside and stretch out towards the refineries at Stanlow where chimneys belch flames and fumes into the heavy air. The pounding and grating of machines emerges from rambling factories, and mingles with the cries of gulls and the splash of waves. Besides the river the A41 to Birkenhead scythes through the communities that grew up by its side. This important road was once the principal route to Liverpool, but since the opening of the second Mersey road tunnel and its link motorways in 1971, it has lost much of its significance.

Below the road the river's course has from time to time been redesigned by engineers and profiteers, and the once-washed sands have thickened into a solution brown and oily. And yet this is the coastline where stories of kings and schemers, of sail and steam, of bustling coaching inns and woodland parks have shared the limelight with tales of great social and industrial adventures and acts of bold speculation. Today, although many of the projects lie sadly abandoned, one may yet discover along these forgotten shores traces of those earlier tempestuous days.

The Chester-Birkenhead road crosses Bromborough Pool. An unfamiliar view of a bridge that hundreds of motorists use every day.
Photograph: Alison Groves

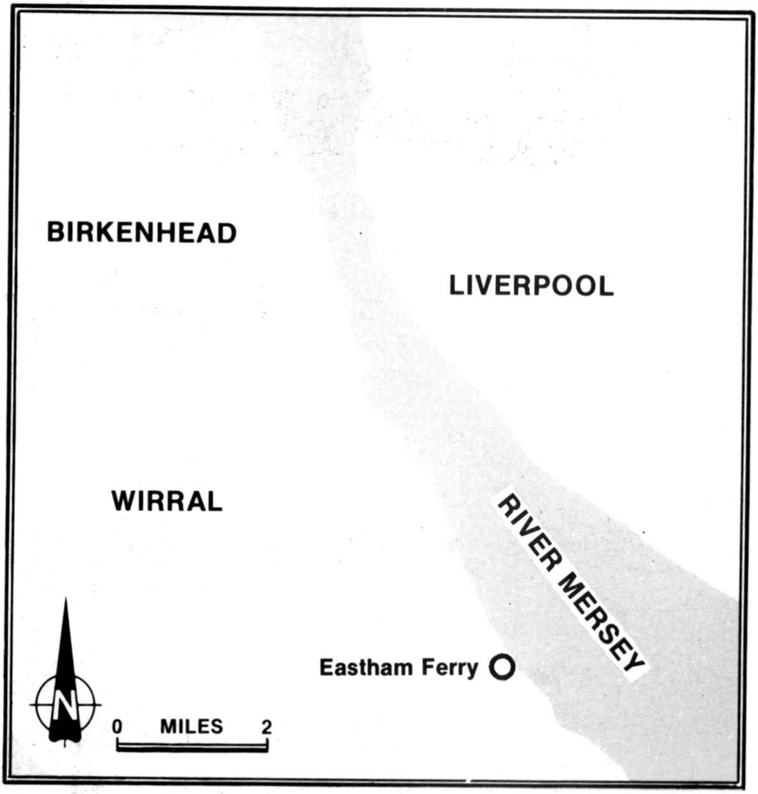

BIRKENHEAD

LIVERPOOL

WIRRAL

RIVER MERSEY

Eastham Ferry ◯

N

0   MILES   2

Chapter One
THE RICHMOND OF CHESHIRE

At Eastham Ferry, in the thick of the industrial maze, there remains a fleeting reminder of how the river bank must have looked before the cranes and pylons cast their shadows. Here it is still possible to stroll along wooded sandstone cliffs against a background of silver and brown birches, broad ferns and witches' brooms — relics of the Royal Forest of Wirral. This rare stretch of sandstone and woodland (practically the only example left along the Mersey shores of Wirral) owes its survival to the Manchester Ship Canal, the construction of which it was thought at the time, would ruin the Ferry and reduce the attractions of its gardens. Ocean-going ships coming in close to the land would, it was argued, disturb the resort's peaceful charm and prevent the ferry boats from maintaining regular services. However, such fears proved to be without foundation, for it was the passage of these Manchester-bound ships that actually inhibited industrial growth in the immediate neighbourhood, and *preserved* much of Eastham's Ferry's sequestered character. The ferry service itself was in fact maintained until 1929, at which time a serious decline in passengers precluded any possibility of survival.

A working coaster, bound for the Manchester Ship Canal passes the woods at Eastham Ferry.   Photograph: Alison Groves

Alarms regarding the durability of Eastham Ferry have regularly been sounded. Just as the late nineteenth century represented a period of concern, so did the 1950s. In 'The Wirral Peninsula' Norman Ellison* adopted a pessimistic approach. He wrote that after 1935, when the ferry pier was finally demolished,

> "Eastham Ferry languished, derelict and almost forgotten, until in 1949 the great oil dock project brought intense activity to the area . . . . . I was there recently and watched giant bulldozers and other mechanical mammoths burying fair green fields under mounds of excavated material; all was noise and bustle. . . . . . The writing is on the wall and it is only a question of time before the woods, the glorious woods carpeted with wild hyacinths and still beautiful, are no more".

By 1980 the picture was very different. "Miraculously Eastham has survived" wrote Alan Brack**" and when I was there the other day you could almost hear the quiet".

In 1847 William Mortimer*** was equally enthusiastic, although he too refers to mixed fortunes.

> "There are few more delightfully situated places in this locality than the immediate vicinity of the ferry, which is within half an hour's sail from the piers of Liverpool. The neighbourhood has long been the favourite resort of many of the denizens of that crowded town, who, while thus enabled to inhale the pure breeze, can participate in picturesque scenery of the finely wooded country by which it is surrounded. An elegant pile of buildings that have recently been erected by Sir William T. Massey Stanley, for an hotel, forms an excellent substitute for the unsightly fabric which previously stood on the margin of the ferry, and the want of accommodation which much impaired the attractions of the village. A new pier, with landing places, is now in course of erection, at which larger and more powerful steam packets will be employed, and a regularity of dispatch insured, that cannot fail to be advantageous. During the summer months the lower woods of Hooton and Brombro' are open to the public, and from present appearances it would seem that Eastham — the Richmond of Cheshire, as it has not infelicitously been called — will rival the glories of its former popularity."

---

*Hale, 1955.
**'The Wirral', Batsford 1980.
***'The History of the Hundred of Wirral', Whittaker & Co., 1847 E.J. Moreton 1972.

But of course in 1847 the ferry was already old. Exactly how old it is impossible to say, for although records date back to 1509 the attention assigned to the area at the time of the eleventh century Doomsday survey would suggest much earlier ferrying activities. Clarification of the extent of these activities is hindered, however, by various changes of name and of siting over the years. In addition to borrowing the name Eastham from the village a mile inland, the ferry was also known as Carlett and as Job's Ferry at different times.

Eastham Village.   Photograph: Lewis's Series. Private Collection

It is still possible to see some vestiges of these earlier landings, the precise location of which changed to accommodate the quirks of shifting channels and sandbanks. For example, close to the present pier (which, together with an iron extension, was erected in 1784 by Messrs. Thomson & Gough), the foundations of a much older structure may be seen at low tide, while 300 yards downstream, partially hidden by a sycamore tree, a flight of twelve steps, deeply cut from the solid cliff face, descends to the water. Below the steps a muddle of large sandstone blocks, the remains of Job's Ferry, still litter the shore.

By the 1800s Eastham Ferry had enjoyed generations, perhaps centuries, of activity. Who can know what strange and primitive craft had carried cargoes of livestock, farm produce and mail, as well as travellers across the half dozen miles to Liverpool, a journey which it was said in 1795 took two and a half hours if conditions were favourable, but could take more than half a day if tides and winds were unco-operative? Who can imagine the excitement that must

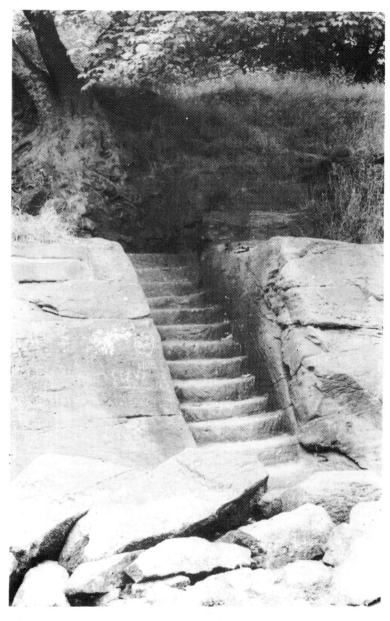

The old steps at Job's Ferry.   Photograph: Alison Groves

Ancient Job's Ferry.   Photograph: Alison Groves

have accompanied the arrival of the fastest coaches in the land, 20 or 30 of which commonly lined the path to the pier waiting to convey businessmen and messengers to Chester, Holyhead, Shrewsbury and far beyond?

For the really capable manager the ferrying business represented a profitable undertaking. It is a popular fact that old Peggy Smith who retired in 1830 after running the steamer services for some years, sat back to enjoy an enormous fortune of £30,000.

A certain Mr.Samuel Smith, "master of the *Eastham Packet*" (a sailing boat), introduced the first steamer, *Princess Charlotte*, as early as 1816. In so doing he inaugurated a steam link with Liverpool that was to last for 113 years, a period in which dozens of boats displayed the Eastham colours. A number of Samuel Smith's subsequent boats were christened in honour of the Stanley family. There was *Lady Stanley, William Stanley, The Old Lady* (a somewhat tactless dedication) and the lord of the fleet, *Sir Thomas Stanley* hewn from the best English oak wood.

The 1830s and the 1840s were not without their misgivings regarding the well-being of the ferry. In 1833 Thomas Brassey's magnificent New Chester Road opened to traffic. This broad, straight highway not only bypassed Eastham village and the ferry, but provided an excellent direct route for coaches from Chester to the short Birkenhead river crossings. In 1840 even more travellers were spirited away from the Eastham terminus with the inauguration of the Chester to Birkenhead railway.

11

It was at this moment that Eastham Ferry began to look to the potential of her attractions as a watering place in order to avert the much feared commercial decline. Far from constituting a period of decay the '40s proclaimed a new era of affluence in the area's history. As we have seen, in 1846 Stanley (according to Mortimer) built his splendid new hotel which, it was said, could seat "upwards of a thousand guests", and laid out his ornamental gardens. Through traffic dwindled but the area took pleasant refuge in meeting the needs of the visitors.

One such visitor was Richard Crompton, Liverpool poet and friend of Charles Dickens, who at one time edited a literary periodical called the 'Liverpool Lantern'. Crompton's romantic poem, 'At Eastham on the Mersey', written in the 1850s celebrated the area's considerable charms.

> A scene of beauty, valley, plain and hill
> Are steeped in golden sunlight. Would that I
> In such a lovely spot could live and die!
> So should my soul of beauty drink its fill
> And of that fullness, through the mind at will
> Put timid blossoms forth; and happily
> At length bear fruit, when from the brightening sky
> Spring smiled upon the earth, my soul would thrill
> To hear the lark's first song, to watch young flowers
> In virgin innocence unfold their leaves
> Through sultry heat to loiter in these bowers
> Beneath their tuneful shade which summer weaves,
> Loving the gifts that bounteous nature showers,
> So should my soul of beauty drink its fill,
> Blooms, music, waving grain, ripe fruit and golden sheaves.
> The summer wind creeps through these peaceful groves
> With happy whisperings of sunny bowers
> Laden with fragrance, languidly it moves
> Faint with perfume borne from a thousand flowers
> Under green boughs of spreading sycamore
> I sit and contemplate this healthful scene,
> The woodland scenery skirting either shore
> And the broad river stretching far between;
> This long green vista, where the elm trees tall,
> Embracing, form an archway overhead,
> Through which, obliquely, broken sunbeams fall,
> And sleep in beauty on the violets' bed.
> No sound is heard, save what the wild birds pour,
> And ripples gushing on the rocky shore.*

*Poem submitted to the present author by Mrs. Bessie Cockburn

Another celebrated visitor was Nathaniel Hawthorne, the American Consul to Liverpool, and author of 'Tanglewood Tales for Girls and Boys', 'The Scarlet Letter' and many other stories. In 1854, the year of his visit to the Eastham Ferry Hotel, Hawthorne was living in Rock Ferry's fashionable Rock Park. He appears to have been very fond of Eastham. In his diary he recorded his affection for the village, favourable impressions of the quality of service at the Ferry Hotel and his appreciation of the views from its principal rooms. Looking north east from the terrace the estuary spreads out like a huge lake. At low tide sandbanks rise from across two miles of still water; troughs and rock pool hollows enhance the feeling of tranquility. Black headed gulls and sea swallows rest and seem to enjoy the calm. As the tide rises again the scene awakens. Red, white and blue pennants flower in the breeze, birds scatter and swoop while voices splinter the silence.

Business boomed. In 1856 the innkeeper and ferry proprietor, Henry Nicholls, inundated by a throng of Good Friday visitors, was substantially fined for the overcrowding of his steamer, the *Eastham Fairy*. It was such hardbitten characters as Nicholls, together with groups of old, yarn-swapping sea captains, breezy companies of strolling entertainers and an unspoilt scenic appeal that gave Eastham Ferry an unusual magnetism that proved all but irresistible to streams of visitors.

The crossing from Liverpool also proved to be a great attraction, and both passengers and locals developed a thorough knowledge of, and strong affection for, the various ferry boats which brough such

Eastham Ferry pier. Photograph: Shurey's Publications. Private Collection.

energy and prosperity to the waterfront. *Loch Lomond* and *Clarence* sailed down from the Clyde. There was *Thomas Royden, Swiftsure* and *Prince Albert* (whose name was changed to *Richmond* in deference to the Ferry's image). There was a *Sprite*, a *Sylph*, and a *Siren*, and a trio of boats from Rock Ferry, *Wasp, Fairy Queen, Gipsey Queen,* their funnels banded in red and black. In the '90s there was the brand new *Athlete* and the old *Onyx* from Harwich. It seems clear that these steamers, each distinctive in habit and appearance, were regarded as living characters rather than inanimate means of transport.

The three most famous characters were undoubtedly *Pearl, Ruby* and *Sapphire* who appeared on the Mersey in 1897-8 and remained on the Eastham run (with the exception of the war years) until 1929 when they were sold for scrap. Their perpendicular, rakeless lines gave the impression that they were both coming and going at the same time, and even in those days of peculiar craft they often caused a raised eyebrow or two.

From the 1840s to the turn the century numerous companies, featuring such notables as William Hillian, Henry Gough, H.M. Lawrence and Thomas Thompson, emerged to conduct the complicated affairs of passage, until in 1897 the EASTHAM FERRY, PLEASURE GARDENS AND HOTEL CO. LTD. was formed to guard the common interests of river and resort.

And so the lovely riverside retreat called and echoed to the sounds of cheerful, sunny crowds. The gentle hills and woodland glades smiled upon and nurtured Victorian and Edwardian diversions.

Picnic at Eastham. Henderson's (Binn's) outing, 1912.
Photograph: Private collection lent by the late Mrs. A. Blackburn

There were intimate family picnics, stylish garden parties, and elaborate entertainments. There were 'boating fiestas', fireworks and treasure hunts. In the woods paths were formed and edged with blocks of sandstone, pits were dug and cages constructed, and a menagerie of bears and lions, elephants and antelopes attracted people from far and near. The fattest lady in the world sat squarely in a precarious wooden shack flanked by a pair of tiny, unsmiling dwarfs. There was a pickled man with two heads next to Monkey Island, and a crocodile from the Nile; a tank of man-eating spiders, and a sea-horse ('the fabulous hippocampus'), said to have been 'landed by a captain from the Mersey during a round-the-world voyage'. There was even a dimly lit mermaid 'from the South'. Above Azalea Dell rapacious visitors queued to throw little red balls at Bonzo, the clown on the trapeze. Hit the spot and his perch would collapse, plunging him into an uninviting well of icy water. There were amazing experiences around every corner. Push a penny into a slot and, at the turn of a handle, one could wonder at moving photographs.

For the truly daring however, there was a terrifying machine contrived from steel trestles and rails called a loop-the-loop, a contraption originating in the amusement park at Atlantic City, U.S.A. in 1901. At Eastham it was publicised as the most frightening and exhilarating ride in the world. In the 'English illustrated Magazine' of December 14, 1901, the machine was described as follows:

> "By means of a loop, which has gained for this supposed pastime the nickname of looping the loop, persons with sufficiently strong nerves are able to ride with their heads downwards at a speed that, at the crucial moment, is said to be 95 mph. The cars cannot run off the rails for they are held down by guard wheels at the sides, so that it is impossible to lift the car from the rails at any point. The weight of the car is carried on a central rail.

> "The car is hauled up a steep incline to a height of 44 feet and then carried round the curve at the top to rush down the right hand slope with such velocity that it is carried by its own momentum up and round the big loop which is egg-shaped not circular.

> "It is when the car is at the highest point of this loop that the passengers ride head downwards. They are strapped in their seats for additional safety."

The car then ran on a further 200 feet swinging into the platform to pick up its next load of courageous passengers. Although the loop-the-loop was fun to watch it proved a little too exhilarating for Eastham tastes and after a short time it had to be dismantled.

Some of those who actually dared to ride the loop, however, retold the tale for many years with great pride. As late as 1963 a certain Mr. R.E. Roberts wrote to the 'Liverpool Echo':

> "Although we had been warned not to go looping the loop Willie Davies and I decided to have a go. We had no difficulty in getting through the pay gate but then we were seen by one of our Sunday School teachers who called out that she would tell our father about it. Fortunately it was too late for her to stop us for the car started up and we were off. A minute later we could proudly boast that we had looped the loop — and what a thrill it was!

> "Then I had to face my father. He must have thought my bravery in tackling the ride meritorious, for he never said a word."

For most people, however, it was easier, and almost as spectacular, to contemplate the courage of others. Blondin, the celebrated Niagara Falls tightrope walker, appeared at Eastham and shared his reputation with a local boy who volunteered to be pushed along the high wire in a fragile wheelbarrow. They said the view form the top was out of this world and no-one was prepared to dispute it!

The heyday of Eastham Ferry came in the decade following the Great War. Liverpool was firmly rooted in the twentieth century. Its harshness and impatience had begun to spread. It was a steamy and fussy place, noisy with trams and motorcars that clattered along the cobbled streets. Working boats crammed its port, while chain-driven steam lorries shrilled and wheezed as did the over-laden shires who threaded their heavy clopping paths along the dock road, bales of cotton, heaps of grain and timbers piled beside their route. Meanwhile, the woods across the estuary — some called them the enchanted woods — represented a different and far more pleasant world. Indeed, the War and the city had combined to transform Eastham's boating lake dipped with trees, the fountain paths and ice cool beers, the open air theatre and the colourful ballroom into a dream.

Pearl, Ruby and *Sapphire* having spent the miserable war years sweeping mines for the Admiralty were now eager to return to their real vocation bearing passengers up river to Eastham. And how the crossing had improved since those early days of sail! Far from being an ordeal for nerve and stomach, these latest boats, stable and reliable, collected their guests at ten past the hour from the Pier Head and deposited them, unperturbed and even elated, before the next hour had rung from the Liver clock tower. The people who appeared so pale and out of sorts in the steep-walled streets of the town invariably took a turn for the better as soon as the decks began to throb beneath their feet. They blushed and blinked as the salty air tightened their cheeks, and strode briskly up the slatted pier, their children scampering behind. Unsociable and taciturn at home, here they would unselfconsciously mingle with the bright young things who had not yet finished dancing away the war clouds. The boys whistled their freedom and sported the symbols of a new, mobile immorality, their shapely motorcars, while the pretty girls, energetic and emancipated, twirled their beads, stream-lined their chests and smiled immodestly.

The Hotel with its bright, spacious verandah buzzed with movement and Mr. Hannaford, the Manager, encouraged, as far as possible, a cosmopolitan clientele and fostered a strongly nautical flavour. Across the road the Vienna Cafe bristled with earnest family groups and flustered waitresses. The Vienna specialised in the most delectable ice creams served in fancy dishes. From the tables outside there was a splendid view of the hotel forecourt and its attractions. For this is where the regimental bands played to attentive audiences. The stern faces of the bandsmen could not disguise their obvious enjoyment in the light relief of such gems as 'Give yourself a pat on the back', and of special military arrangements of King Oliver's 'High Society' and Arthur Sullivan's 'Pair of sparkling eyes'. The Charleston and Cachucha made happy companions. The audiences themselves were dotted with brigadiers, captains and majors, whose chests swelled with hard-earned pride. After the concert many would wander down to see the gypsies and to sample their jangling bobby horses and swingboats. Others swarmed through the great Triumphal Arch, which had been erected in honour of Queen

Eastham Ferry Hotel and Gardens. The Triumphal Arch was built to celebrate Queen Victoria's Golden Jubilee.
Photograph: Valentines. Private Collection

Victoria's Golden Jubilee (and which housed the pay box to the gardens), to applaud Granville Hope's 'Merry Madcaps . . . Unique . . . Versatile . . . Refined'. Mothers and fathers happily abandoned their children while they themselves settled down to marvel at Goldy's lightning smoke sketches of local scenes, to gasp at Mr. Mystery's magic, to join in their favourite tunes with Crystal and Miss Melody (whose speciality was the beguiling 'Where do flies go in the wintertime?'), and to laugh until they cried at the antics of Beeky the clown (who twenty-five years later became Jackson Earle, 'the guv'nor' of New Brighton's popular 'Melody Inn').

Yet tastes and styles are fickle. Fortunes change.

As the '20s drew to a close ruffians gathered in the woods at weekends to ridicule and intimidate respectable visitors. They surged through the gardens in rowdy bands and rejoiced in scratching paintwork, breaking glass and twisting railings.

As we have seen, steamer services were withdrawn in 1929, but that was not quite the end of things. In 1930 Wallasey Ferries announced in the local press that they would include Eastham calls in their summer schedule.

"A new feature of this season's service of river cruises will be daily calls at Eastham, the ordinary service to which has been suspended, allowing the whole aftenoon ashore for rambles in the woods or through the lovely countryside, or for sports in the recreation grounds."

"Although the EASTHAM FERRY AND HOTEL COMPANY are not running a ferry service this season, it is hoped they will resume the service in the future."

The experiment failed to attract sufficient passengers and was abandoned, yet although the FERRY AND HOTEL COMPANY was unable to re-introduce regular services, Eastham was reluctant to admit defeat. In fact, in 1933 a bold venture entitled the *NEW LIVERPOOL-EASTHAM FERRY AND HOTEL COMPANY LTD.*, initiated what in the event turned out to be a final bout of advertising. In newspapers, journals, on hoardings and letterheads the company announced:

76 ACRES OF PLEASURE GROUNDS

with

Large Dancing Pavilion

AMUSEMENTS OF ALL KINDS

DAILY SAILINGS FROM GEORGE'S STAGE
REGULAR HOURLY SERVICE
from
11.10 a.m. to 9.10 p.m. (last boat)
extra afernoon boat

MAGNIFICENT WOODS
CHARMING WALKS
SCHOOL PICNICS
and
Any Kind of PLEASURE PARTY catered for
FIELD FOR SPORTS

Frequent al fresco ENTERTAINMENTS
in
PUBLIC GARDEN
BOWLS

CIRCULAR MOTOR TOURS arranged through WIRRAL

RESIDENTIAL HOTEL and PRIVATE GARDENS
HIGH CLASS CATERING
at
HOTEL AND CAFES

GARAGE for MOTORS and CYCLES

Special facilities for
TERRITORIAL WEEK-END CAMPS, SCOUTS etc.-

In truth, however, there was a sense of unreality surrounding the company's aspirations. For one thing, the pier was by now considered sufficiently hazardous to Canal shipping to warrant demolition and, for another, the Gardens themselves were not quite what they had been. The zoological collection had been dispersed, successful maintenance of the theatre and various restaurants had become a financial burden and, in any case, presentations of pierrots and concert parties seemed frivolous and irrelevent in the cynical climate of the '30s. The great Triumphal Arch, gateway to the whole spectacle, had begun to disintegrate from neglect. As it did so, splinters of wood and fragments of plaster dropped from it, destroying forever the illusion of permanence it had so effortlessly and convincingly created. To add the final blow, the beautiful ballroom was burnt to ashes.

A period of neglect and consequent decay descended upon the Gardens and lasted for more than a generation. Tangled undergrowth crept over the pathways and hid the last traces of the ruined ballroom and lake. The remains of the theatre were torn down and the deep bear pit was filled with rubble. Only the Hotel and Pier Bar (both of which remained open during these otherwise dismal years) hinted at the resort's former glories: for the rest of the dream had faded. In the meantime industrial developments continued to reach out towards the Ferry and the construction of the 18-acre Queen Elizabeth Oil Dock appeared to offer a special threat to the abandoned waterfront.

Eastham Ferry Gardens: the old fountain.   Photograph: Alison Groves

Yet, surprisingly, the woods held their ground until 1970 when, as a contribution to European Conservation Year, the area was designated a Country Park 'to be preserved and enhanced for generations to come'. Under the auspices of Wirral Borough Council (together with the Cheshire Conservation Trust and various local history societies) diseased and dangerous trees were replaced to provide a varied and natural habitat for the bird and animal life, and a nature trail was designed to take advantage of the changing scenes of river and woodland. A visitors' centre with interesting displays and information about the countryside was opened to the public, and picnic areas and car parks were laid out overlooking the ancient sandstone cliffs.In the gardens themselves, Azalea Dell was trimmed and replanted and the bear pit and ornamental fountains were excavated.

In 1978-9 the Hotel and Pier Bar were refurbished and a new restaurant, the Ferry Tavern, was opened. Although the Hotel's old wooden-framed verandah was removed, the lounge with its velvet curtains and original brass fittings maintained something of its Victorian flavour and served as a timely remainder of Eastham's halcyon past. The new publicity, too, had a familiar ring. The development boasted 'a large play area in an enclosed garden with swings and slides for the youngsters to amuse themselves, while dad and mum enjoy a drink at one of the shaded tables'. A programme of further improvements was undertaken in the '80s when the Pier Bar was supplanted by the Nelson Bistro, and the interior of the Hotel was re-planned.

Against all the odds Eastham Ferry had begun a new chapter in a remarkable story.

Eastham Ferry Hotel.
Photograph: Alison Groves

21

BIRKENHEAD

LIVERPOOL

WIRRAL

Bromborough Pool Village O

RIVER MERSEY

N

0   MILES   2

Chapter 2
THE MYTHICAL MR. PRICE

Not more than two miles downstream from Eastham Ferry the modest waters of the Dibbin Brook drain into Bromborough Pool and spread outwards into Lever's deep water dock. Along the shadowy course of the Dibbin the dale is rich and green. Wooded slopes, reaching from Eastham, afford glimpses of rocky outcrops and meadows. And yet, between the leaves, one may also see corrugated walls and soaring tanks glinting silver in the sun. Irregular trailing boughs contrast starkly with disciplined ranks of barrels and drums of perhaps tallow or cottonseed oil. There are high buildings made of windows, and steel rails busy with trucks and diesel locomotives. The air is a blend of sweet bark, damp ferns, tangy breezes from the river and, occasionally, flurries of vinegary chemicals that take the breath away.

For this is known as Unilever country, a land of Sunlight and detergents, of silos and overhead supply pipes, of beautiful half-timbered houses, Diamonds and Dells and green lawns.

Farther down the Pool around the elbow of the Sunlight Canal, however, lie the forgotten reminders of an earlier, though less spectacular, operation than Lever's. Here, a row of rotten mud-locked barges clings to the old bank of the inlet and a disused wharf leads to a factory and to a village that was throbbing with life at least a generation before the dawn of Lever's day. For though William Lever's magnificent achievements have rightly earned for him historical acclaim, the inital development of the Bromborough Pool site belongs in reality not to him but to the Wilson family whose accomplishments have remained, comparatively speaking, in the shadows. Yet it was James Wilson who, in 1853, discovered the Pool and who confirmed its industrial and social potential by establishing a northern branch of Price's Patent Candle Company of Battersea, together with a self-contained village for the company employees.

As late as 1931, with the virtual completion of the dock, Bromborough Pool was "discovered " for a third time and the "Manchester Commercial Guardian" of 30th April devoted an entire edition to the project. "This new rural estate" it said, "addresses its appeal to businesses which desire breathing space, clean layouts and clear courses for development," and especially to those appreciating the advantages of "a bracing peninsula where there is no smoke-laden atmosphere to fatigue the worker and contaminate the product."

Bromborough Pool today with an old barge, and, in the background, Prices original Factory Tower.
Photograph: Alison Groves

William Wilson, Founder of Price's.
Photograph: Private Collection

It is true that the dock (the story of which we shall relate in our next Chapter) transformed the Pool from an unimposing terminal for barges to an international port capable of handling ocean-going ships. But to the Wilson community much of this "Guardian" talk was a thrice-told tale. For to them this had always been known as Price's country, a land of candles and molasses, cricket matches and prize silver bands.

Who, then, was this Mr. Price whose name had become synonymous by the mid-1850s, with industrial excellence and social consciousness of the most enlightened kind? It was Mr. Price who had preserved an element of humanity in a tough industrial world, who had taken his workers out of tightly packed conurbations and had placed them in decent houses; Mr. Price who, it was argued, had shown to the avaricious world of commerce an acceptable side of capitalism. The truth is, however, that Mr. Price did not actually exist. He was, like so many features in the early history of the Candle Company, a brainchild of William Wilson, the Company's founder.

Following the failure of his father's iron works in Scotland, William had moved to London in 1812. There he soon impressed the capital's business fraternity with his diligence and enterprise. In 1830 he entered into partnership with a certain Mr. Lancaster — an arrangement which resulted in the setting up of a coconut pressing factory in Battersea — and, in order to avoid a "loss of dignity" which may have accompanied the use of their own names, they borrowed the title "E. Price" from Lancaster's aunt, a lady who could claim no association whatever with the company. When Mr. Lancaster withdrew in 1847 William Wilson and his sons, James and George, gained control of what was by then a flourishing candle manufacturing plant, and changed the name to "Edward Price and Company"*.

And yet Mr. Price took on a life of his own. Even William Makepeace Thackeray in his novel "The Virginians" (1857-59) was moved to lament the "Horrible guttering tallow (that) smoked and stunk in passages", and to bless the celebrated "Mr. Price and all other Luciferous benefactors of mankind" for banishing to antiquity such primitive methods of lighting. Indeed, Edward Price became such an important figure it was fashionable in some sectors of London society to profess to have met him - even to have dined with him - a habit which must have caused some amusement in the Wilson household.

Soon the much fabled gentleman and his Patent Candle Company were so successful that it became necessary in the early 1850s to embark upon a policy of expansion. In the event James and George

---

*From: "Still the Candle Burns" (Price's Patent Candle Co. 1947, reprinted 1972).

Wilson, who were now responsible for the business's fortunes, resolved to explore regions other than cholera-ridden London. A number of factors appeared to suggest Liverpool which had become the principal centre for the handling of palm oil, an essential ingredient in the manufacture of candles. But in some instances Liverpool's social afflictions were, if anything, even more serious than those encounted in London, and the last thing the brothers wanted was to become entangled in another diseased environment. And so they turned away from Liverpool and decided to consider the Wirral shores.

By this time one or two companies had already been established around Birkenhead but there remained miles of the Wirral coast that had conceded nothing in the name of progress. In his search for an appropriate site along the fringes of the Mersey, James Wilson, an elegant figure complete with top hat and cane, must have created a bizarre impression striding across the mud flats, surveying the lie of the Eastham Marshes and the caves at Wallasey, or clambering over rust-coloured cliffs as yet unstained by industrial endeavour. His final choice, Bromborough Pool, was a triumph of perception and courage.

True, the chosen estate was quite inexpensive but, isolated from villages and ferry routes, it hardly constituted a bargain. The nearest hamlet lay beyond the marl pits of Rice Woods on Magazine Shore, while the more substantial settlements of Bromborough and New Ferry were two rugged miles away. Indeed, apart from its clean atmosphere, the site's only advantage was its potential link with the port across the estuary.

Initially Mr. Mainwaring, the lord of Bromborough manor, was unimpressed by the prospects of a factory on his land and refused to sell, although he did offer the Wilsons a long-term lease. At this time, however, an article which appeared in "Quarterly Review" stressing the social aspects of the scheme changed Mainwaring's mind. His imagination was so fired by the idea of a progressive village on his own doorstep that he agreed to release for sale 42 acres of agricultural land belonging to Court House Farm. An initial survey of the area, however, revealed that some parts of the land were swampy and watery. Consequently a further 19 acres were made available for development in the summer of 1853. The entire 61 acre site cost Mr. Price's Company £12,267 10s 0d., and excavation and construction began immediately after signing of the contract on 2nd August 1853.

* * * * * * * *

Although model villages were still something of a novelty the Wilsons themselves were already veterans in the art of "community development". However, it was neither the brothers James and George, nor even their father, William, who were the family innovators in this field. Indeed, it was William's own father, John, who must take much of the credit. The tradition of Wilsonian altruism, then, stretched back beyond Bromborough, beyond even the so-called Belmont works at Battersea, to a small village called Wilsontown in late eighteenth century Lanarkshire. During those years momentous changes were taking place both at home and abroad. In Britain the industrial revolution had given birth to new processes of mass production which had generated in turn mass employment and mass exploitation and squalor. Abroad Clive, Hastings, Cook and Nelson roamed the world waving the not altogether philanthropic banner of British superiority. Britain was rich and arrogant, powerful and tyrannical, but she did not entirely lack a self-critical and humanitarian streak. Both ends of the scale were heavily weighted and the mansions of the rich were depressingly counter-balanced by some of the worst slums in the world.

In 1784, however, David Dale, a Glasgow linen merchant, had established near the Falls of Clyde, a water-powered cotton mill together with some dwellings for his workers. During the next decade he built three more mills in the steep wooded gorge in addition to comfortable houses for 1,000 people. He called his village New Lanark. In 1799 Robert Owen inherited New Lanark and its factories, expanded opportunties for leisure and education and, with judicious publicity, made it famous. The Wilson family lived only a few miles across the hills and often visited Owen's estate. The Wilsons, shrewd and humane, must have been excited by the pleasant, healthy atmosphere, and the influence this appeared to have on the efficiency of the business.

Despite a lack of true industrial experience John Wilson opened his own factory in 1781, when ironstone had been discovered on the high, windblown hills. Soon, according to the "Hamilton Advertiser" in which a retrospective feature appeared in 1938*, "there sprang up on the banks of the Mouse stream . . . a living hive of industry in whose furnaces and forges cold raw materials . . . were transformed and fashioned by the conquering ingenuity of man into a variety of goods for the markets of the world".

The village of Wilsontown, which was established, like New Lanark, to house the workers, grew up beside the foundry on a high ridge approached by primitive tracks. Standing 900 feet above sea level this remote outpost of Lanarkshire was surrounded by the

*The Romance of Wilsontown, Aug. 1938.

*One of John Wilson's
impressiver houses in
Wilson town, Lanark
shire. (1977).*
Photographs:
    Maurice Hope

*New Lanark on the
Falls of Clyde.*

Wilson town today.

28

Pentland Hills, Coulter Fell and Mount Tinto and was unprotected by either wood or fold from the wild upland conditions.

The dwellings themselves were sufficiently substantial, however, to withstand the foulest gales, built as they were of stone and lime. Indeed, a number of the original houses were still inhabited in the 1930s,

"the most striking example of this being the old and well known Quality Row which, previous to being closed for human habitation in the year 1936, housed no fewer than 174 souls. Two storeys in height this famous row occupied a commanding position looking down on the works, and what hosts of men, woman and children from generation to generation during its long period of usefulness were happy to call it their home.

"The old school still stands as if defying time, although it is now in a ruinous state. On the lintels of the doorways of this ancient house of learning, carved out some eight score years ago for the edification of all who might pass within its portals, can still be read the two great divine commands: FEAR GOD and LOVE THY NEIGHBOUR."

Within those forbidding walls generations of children were taught to read and write at a nominal charge, and those who showed promise were even encouraged to pursue a broader curriculum.

In addition to Quality Row and the school there were other buildings in the village of Wilsontown, notably the single storey of Red Row and, dominating the busy scene, an impressive Mansion House for members of the Wilson family themselves. It was down the steps of this house that John Wilson passed when the business eventually failed. He took with him, according to local reports, "only the apparel which he wore, the walking stick he carried in his hand" and his son William. With the collapse of the Company the Wilsons were ruined, but perhaps they were partly consoled by virtue of the fact that they had at least left their old employees with a community to call their own.

It was at this point that William moved to London to use as best he could whatever talent he might possess.

* * * * * * * *

William Wilson enjoyed a high measure of success in the development of his new Battersea company and its various facilities. His sons, James and George, were enthusiastically involved in the

Two views of Bromborough Pool village.
Photographs: Alison Groves

venture. James established a school to help lead children towards the Christian life, while George offered books as prizes for outstanding pupils. An allotment scheme was also initiated by George, cricket matches were established to counter the threat of cholera, and outings by steamer to the sea were occasionally arranged. Such experience stood the brothers in good stead when they opened their Bromborough works.

Indeed, by the time the Bromborough project was under way, the Company Board itself had agreed to support that strange "mixture of idealism, religious belief, common sense and business sense that governed the Wilsons". (Alan Watson, "Price's Village"). From the outset the brothers were determined that their village should incorporate high quality housing and pleasant social and recreational features. Cottages were scrupulously designed and built by Julian Hill of London (who worked in close contact with the Wilsons themselves). Each dwelling would incorporate the most up to date sanitation and sewerage; gardens to the front and rear would provide areas for cultivation and relaxation; and the community itself would include a chapel, a hospital, school, village hall, library, sports grounds and playgrounds. Such elaborate and carefully planned facilities were not to be enjoyed elsewhere until almost forty years later with the development of Port Sunlight.

In the summer of 1854 thirteen of the Company's Battersea employees, selected especially for their qualities of leadership and initiative, moved to Bromborough Pool Village and settled in their new cottages on York Street. Their duties were threefold: to provide essential industrial continuity, to welcome the new employees who arrived with the completion of Manor Place, and to encourage the growth of a strong communal life. By 1858 Mr. Price's Village could boast seventy-six houses, a hostel and a population of 460.

The Wilsons themselves interfered as little as possible in the foundations of institutions, believing that the impetus should come from those who lived in the village. Their influence, however, was nonetheless strongly evident. James gave his indelible stamp to the Mutual Improvement Society with its somewhat pompous aims "to promote generally the intellectual, moral and social advancement of its members". His ideals were also discernible in the daily ten minute prayer meetings that were held in the open air each breakfast time (five minutes of which took place in the Company's time, five minutes in the employees'). The cricket club was also encouraged by James, as was the strongly moral campaign against gambling and drinking (a campaign which the village's small co-operative store contrived to side-step by selling Wrexham ales from behind a high wooden screen!). On the other hand, George's passion for gardening (he was awarded no fewer than 25 certificates by the Royal Horticultural Society for his cultivation of lilies!) was evident in the provision of personal allotments on Company land and in the foundation of what was to become a highly distinguished and inveterate Horticultural Society. The Mutual Improvement and Horticultural Societies were founded within two years of the opening of the village, and a host of other organisations, covering wide areas of interest, followed as the list below illustrates.

1854   Mutual Improvement Society

1854   Industrial Provident Society

1855   Horticultural Society

1855   Cricket Club

1856   Band

1860   Football Club

1867   Child's Club

1869   Sick and Funeral Society

1890   Housing Society

1896   Mother's Union

1897   Bowling Club

1901   Dramatic Society

1918   Fur and Feather Society

1918   Miniature Rifle Club

1920   Gymnastic Club

1920   Swimming Club

1921   League of Nations

1925   Hockey Club

1926   Tennis Club

1929   Badminton Club

1948   Pensioners' Club

1961   Youth Club

1962   Motoring Club

In addition to these societies there were numerous church groups (such as the Lads' Guild, a Bible Class, Boys' Club, Senior and Junior Girls' Classes and so on) and the celebrated Volunteer Corps of 1859 which mustered in response to the threats from Napolean III. The Corps (which became attached to the 4th Company of Cheshire Rifles in 1861) took part in the Duke of Cambridge's magnificent review of 12,000 Volunteers held at Sefton Park, Liverpoool, in 1867.

It was not all plain sailing, however. Despite their initial support for the Wilson's social visions, Mr. Price's shareholders were not altogether happy. Early in 1856 it was noted that the previous year's cost relating to educational and religious instruction had amounted to no less than £8,600. During 1858 the Board met to investigate what they called "extravagant expenditure on education and recreation", expenditure thought to be particularly prodigal in view of the commercial decline of that year. And this was not the first time the brothers had been reprimanded. On a previous occasion they were curtly informed that it was certainly "not the business of the Company to promote Christianity" and sporting festivals. Yet, at the same time, the Board was compelled to be diplomatic, for the Wilsons were outstanding industrialists and managers who, despite their philanthropic eccentricities, could hardly have been accused of indulging themselves in community-making at the expense of the Company. Between 1854 and 1858, for example, George had ensured the Company's solvency by devising revolutionary processes of manufacture. (One of his major discoveries, the purification of glycerine by distillation in a current of steam was ultimately found to have many uses both industrial and medicinal, and it was primarily for his work in this field that George Wilson was elected a Fellow of the Royal Society). In order to pacify the Board, however, the Wilsons offered their resignations. Not surprisingly these were not accepted but, nevertheless, the Board did determine to exercise "a more real and efficient control" over affairs in future.

It was not until 1873 that a modest new building phase began. In that year South View, the village's third street, was laid parallel to Manor Place and York Street, alongside Price's quarry. Although only half a dozen houses were built at this stage, the ground plan of the village was now substantially completed. Further progress was frustrated by a series of events culminating when flood water rose from the quarry and caused subsidence as far as the factory. The remaining houses of South View were in fact delayed for another twenty years. By the '90s, however, when domestic development began again, the offending quarry had been filled in, and in its place stood a field of neat allotments, which were rented out to tenants for 6d a year. Apart from two fine Georgian residences (one of which has recently been demolished) which were built overlooking the cricket pitch, these new houses were the most spacious of all the village properties. Built of red brick and attractively gabled, the South View houses appeared to reflect the influence of the growing village of Port Sunlight a short distance away.

As for the public buildings, priority was given to educational facilities. The village's first purpose-built school was opened in 1858. (Before that date classes had been held in the Iron House, a building inside the works). The headmistress was a certain Miss Humble who "had two ladies as assistant teachers". Alan Wilson relates that

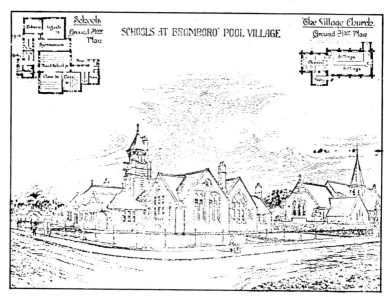

Bromborough Pool: the school and church. Price's. Private Collection

discipline was no real problem, for when "their didactic and feminine skills failed to keep order and impart knowledge, the brawny aid of the Assistant Works Manager was called on to provide corporal punishment".

By the 1880s the school was bursting at the seams and a new building, made of sandstone from the Company's quarry, was opened in January 1899. The old building, with its curved roof and high windows, became the village hall.

As we have seen, the religious traditions of Wilsontown and Battersea were continued at Bromborough — indeed it was unthinkable that a man who could compose such pious tracts as "Ignorance of Sin. Very blind eyes opened" as James had done, should allow moral instruction to deteriorate. Yet it was not until 1890, ironically the year of James's death, that a church was opened. The event was signalled by the salutory firing of a cannon and a healthy rendition of "Onward Christian Soldiers" led by the band. Dedicated to St. Matthew by the Bishop of Chester, the building contains an interesting link with the company's southern origins, for the alter rests upon a set of oak balusters from Cardinal Wolsey's Battersea residence. Soon the church could summon a choir of forty singers, and· the building was barely large enough for the congregations it regularly attracted.

At the turn of the century the community was in full swing. 728 people strolled the bright streets and a handsome lodge guarded the village's private identify, as did the custom of closing the estate to the public one day a year. Weekend dances, concerts, fairs on the green, colourful horticultural shows and frequent productions staged by the Dramatic Society in the village hall permeated the community with an extraordinary vitality and sense of purpose.

The cricketers, however, were perhaps the village's most popular heroes. Alan Watson tells the story of the foundation of the Club*. As early as 1856

> "the Mutual Improvement Society asked Price's to give £10 towards buying cricket tackle, and with this twelve bats, twenty-four balls and some gloves were purchased. In the same year the Company paid for the seeding of a cricket pitch on the village recreation ground. This lay on the bank of the River Mersey and the hundreds of spectators who turned up to watch matches had a magnificent view for miles up and down the river and of Liverpool on the opposite shore.

> "There must have been little time to take in the view, however, for the matches were often exciting and the fixtures between the Bromborough team and that from the factory at Battersea raised keen interest and great feelings of local patriotism".

The cricket team achieved famous victories all over Merseyside and on one occasion the first eleven, playing away from home, beat Oxton in an important cup competition. Local legend has it that during the afternoon an urgent message was rushed to the village: "Oxton all out for 23. Please send the band".

"Mr. Price's gentlemanly football team" also recorded some fine results. They met Everton in the 1870s, won the Liverpool F.A. Medal in 1884, and enhanced a glowing reputation by excellent performances in the new leagues.

With the dawn of the twentieth century, much to Mr. Price's chagrin, the revolutionary incandescent gas mantle seriously began to affect the supremacy of the candle, a situation which resulted in a period of financial uncertainty for the Company. Under such circumstances it would have been inappropriate to embark upon new building projects. Indeed, apart from the completion of the hospital, the provision of a gate near Rice Woods to prevent cows from straying onto the cricket square, and the erection of a memorial after the Great War, no further developments were undertaken.

---

*Price's Village.

Mr. Price's cricket team.   Photograph: Price's. Private Collection

The Bromborough Dock scheme of 1931 held far-reaching consequences for both the village and the Company. With its completion the community was cut off from the river bank for the first time in its eighty year history. An immense embankment packed with rocks and silt lined the river forming a long artificial waterfront. The village green, from where cricket balls had often splashed into the Mersey, found itself far inland as designers provided hundreds of acres of new, unnatural meadows. Slowly buildings and machinery surrounded the streets: a storage tank depot blocked their northern outlook and tall factories rose in the east. As for the Company itself, in 1936 the proximity of the Lever empire was rationalised when Price's Patent Candles joined forces with Unilever to become Price's Chemicals Ltd. (There have, of course , been further changes since then).

After the Second World War the village chapel and its societies experienced a gradual decline, yet Price's impressive sporting traditions have remained very much alive. Cricket and football have flourished in recent years as has the Sports and Social Club which continues to introduce new ideas to meet modern tastes. As in days gone by, however, the village's foremost social event is still the Horticultural Society's Flower and Vegetable Show.

Yet in terms of social activities and of physical dimensions, Price's Village has shrunk considerably in the last twenty years. During the 1960s the old lodge, the shop, and almost one third of the cottages were demolished in order to allow for expansion of the works and to ensure the preservation of an effective safe area between factory and community. 1986 has witnessed a new programme of demolition. The population has aged, a problem which is reflected in the plight of the village school. At the close of the 1970s only nine of the school's ninety five pupils came from Bromborough Pool. It is a dilemma for which there is no solution.⁻

Perhaps, then, with the young settling farther afield, it is only a matter of time before Price's Village, so affectionately fostered by James and George Wilson, not to mention the mythical Mr. Price himself, will disappear into the archives of social history.

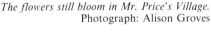
The flowers still bloom in Mr. Price's Village.
Photograph: Alison Groves

One evening in 1864 when T.C. Wright, Chairman of Price's, was dining with W.H. Smith (of bookshop fame) who was at the time First Lord of the Admiralty, Wright noted that the menu card bore a drawing of a ship in full sail. When Wright showed the menu to James Wilson he, Wilson, was so impressed that he acquired the idea for the Company. Soon afterwards the ship in full sail became the worldwide symbol for Price's.

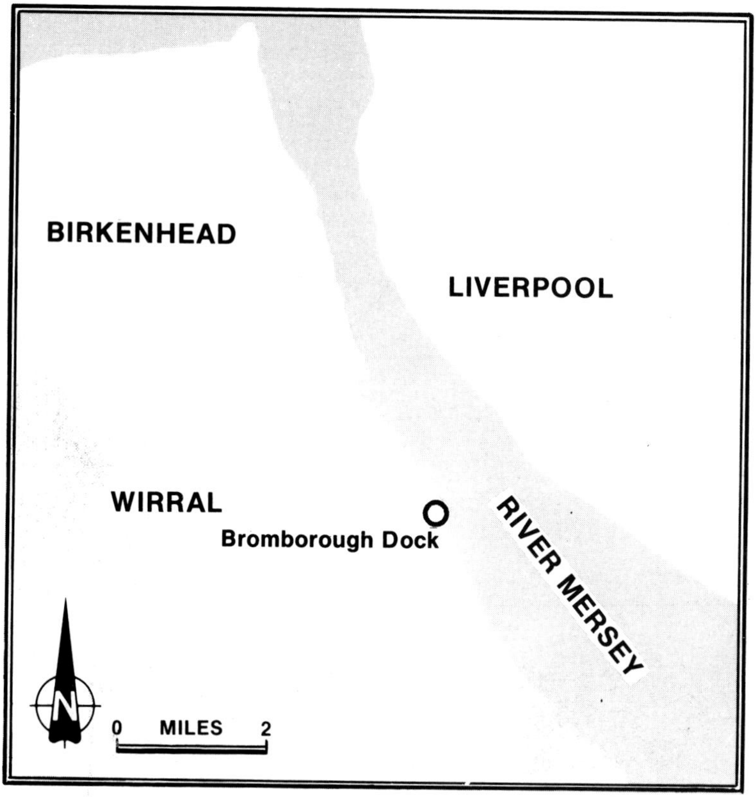

BIRKENHEAD

LIVERPOOL

WIRRAL
Bromborough Dock

RIVER MERSEY

N

0   MILES   2

Chapter 3
A GREAT ENTERPRISE

In shaping society's habits the energetic industrialists who developed the Wirral shores exerted a potent influence not only upon their workforces, but on the very geography of the estates they governed. This was especially so in cases where those estates held access to the valuable river highway, and it is not surprising to discover that the Lairds, the Wilsons and the Levers defined not only the course of social and industrial history but redefined the course of the Mersey.

At the same time, however, the Mersey estuary was not easily managed. Its powerful tidal swell and fall, as well as its assertive currents dictated that cargo handling and ship repairs could only be negotiated behind the custodial walls of costly and complicated impounded docks.

Bromborough Dock was a late comer to the Mersey scene. This vast private enterprise was one of the numerous consequences of William Hesketh Lever's expanding commercial interests. The completion of such a project would provide Lever Brothers' Port Sunlight factory (established in the 1880s) with a self contained international port, and a direct link with the company's tropical plantations and whaling activities. The dock was far from finished

Cottage Homes, Park Road, Port Sunlight.

Port Sunlight village. Photograph: Lever Brothers Ltd. Private Collection

when Lord Leverhulme (who had been created a Viscount in 1922) died in 1925, yet it confirms, as do many other features of his remarkable career, the comprehensive ambition of the great industrialist who began his working life by cutting up bars of soap in his father's grocery shop in Bolton. The setting up of Bromborough Port represents the tiniest fragment in the achievement of the man who created both Port Sunlight and a vast industrial empire but it is nevertheless that Port project that we shall summarise here.

On Friday, October 31st, 1924, the 'Port Sunlight News' briefly reviewed some of the wider accomplishments of the company before going on to describe the dock scheme itself:

> "We have received a copy of the souvenir isssued by Messrs. Lever Bros., which gives fine views of Port Sunlight, the model city of the world. Views of the huge works, docks and their annexes, show the ramifications of this wonder firm in various parts of the world. The whole thing is astounding. Nothing that can make for the comfort and well-being of the armies of workers has been overlooked. Port Sunlight alone must represent a gigantic expenditure. It is beautiful to behold, and in the various countries where works have been established the same care for humanity has been taken. This is a side of capitalism of which the general public ought to know a great deal more than they do."

A description of the proposed dock scheme followed.

> "The entire works cover an area of some 145 acres on the foreshore of the Mersey and have a frontage on the river of about $1\frac{1}{4}$ miles. .

> "The dock has a deep water area of about 18 acres and includes three quays of a total length of 2,400 feet. The approach from the river consists of a short dredged channel leading to the entrance lock 75 feet in width and having a clear length of 120 feet between the caissons. The depth of water over the lock sill will be 36 feet at high water ordinary spring tides, and 27 feet at high water neap tides. Two timber jetties, 190 feet and 240 feet long respectively, are provided outside the lock entrance for the assistance of vessels entering the dock ... On the south side of the dock the frontage line of the works will be formed by a mass concrete wall, 3,400 feet long behind which a reclamation amounting to about 50 acres will be gradually carried out. On the north side the frontage line is formed by a rubble embankment about 2,000 feet long containing an area to be reclaimed of 52 acres."

And so at a time when the construction of docks and factories was a tangible manifestation of growing affluence every stage of the programme was followed with impatient enthusiasm.

The first step was the construction of massive embankments so that 'dry' work could begin as soon as possible. Conditions were arduous and during these early stages progress was halted with every incoming tide. Indeed even when the waters had receded the working trenches had to be pumped out and tons upon tons of silt carted away before further headway could be made. Another early task was the excavation of service channels so that existing barge traffic to Price's and Lever Brothers' should suffer as little disruption as possible. Many experts forecast defeat in these initial stages but the sceptics reckoned without the marvellous steam shovels of a certain Mr. Ruston.

It was reported in the 'Manchester Guardian' that in these extremely adverse circumstances:

> "two No. 6 Ruston steam shovels, mounted on caterpillar tracks, were used to take out the rocks . . . Each time the water left, the channel and the railway tracks were covered with black mud. It was soon found that little progress could be made if valuable working time was taken up in moving the diggers in and out of the channel, and the practice of leaving the navvies at their working faces when the tides rose had to be adopted. Twice daily the machines were submerged until only the tops of the funnels and the jibs could be seen, and there is on record a description of a collision between a barge and a steam navvy which must surely be unique . . . That these machines suffered little harm from this most unusual and, from a mechanical point of view, very unfair treatment, is proved by the fact that later they excavated the railway approach cutting and . . . the huge dock basin."

Machines feature as often as their masters in press reports of the operation. There was the story of locomotive No. 522, the 'Sunlight', the first loco to be used when the factory itself had been founded. It worked for nearly 30 years at the soap works before being sold to a colliery in the North East. Sold again to public contractors No. 552 eventually found itself back at Port Sunlight under the name of 'Mick'. After 40 years of service Mick was still the sturdiest and most sought after locomotive on the job.

However, to return to the excavation of the main basin. Most of the reports relating to the stages of construction and the measures adopted to solve formidable problems are necessarily of a highly technical nature and are hardly within the province of this chapter.

Suffice it to say that in April 1928 the voluminous waters of the river were finally excluded from the enclosed area and the dock excavation commenced. Men still sank to their thighs in dark mud and silt, and side-tip wagons (built by the Wigan Wagon Company!) were regularly derailed as were the engines that slithered down the slimy banks, but with painstaking care enormous locks and towering caissons were fitted, temporary arched dams were demolished and by September 22nd, 1930, the basin was set to receive its full complement of Mersey waters. In February 1931 the freighter *Nigerian* sailed in with 3500 tons of palm kernels on board.

It remained only to celebrate, and celebrate they did. The great opening ceremony took place on Friday 17th April, 1931, an occasion to remember, and 'Progress', the Unilever* Company magazine, resolved to savour every moment.

"The sixty seconds between a quarter and fourteen minutes to eleven of the morning of Friday, 17th April, 1931, will be remembered by Port Sunlight among the most intensely crowded moments of its history," the magazine declared. "During that minute the Bromborough Dock was opened by the President of the Board of Trade.

"Modern industrial inaugurations can be prosaic enough events, but whenever they touch the sea or ships glamour overtakes them. Thus a launching remains one of the most exciting occasions we have inherited from the past . . . That same surge of glamour came upon everybody assisting at the dock opening as the White Star tender *Magnetic*, with a distinguished company of guests on board, sailed through the lock and cut with her bows the red, white and blue ribbon stretched across the dock entrance.

"Everyone suddenly burst out cheering . . . with the spontaneous impulse of a great body of people lifted out of all individual reserve and compelled to acclaim vocally a stirring experience.

" 'The sun and the rain were flying', the flags stood out straight in the stiff breeze, exploding maroons set up a chorus of sound which the sirens of ships and barges prolonged, overhead a small aeroplane appeared from out of the clouds and dipped in salute, school children on the wharf released their carnival streamers excitedly, and the band of the Lancashire and National Sea Training

---

*In 1929 the Unilever organisation was established when Lever Brothers amalgamated with a group of Dutch companies.

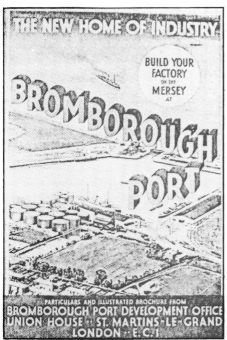

This poster, published in 1932, helped to promote Bromborough Port.

Bromborough Dock, 1950.

Photograph: Private Collection

Homes struck up 'God Save the King'. So many things happened at once that one pair of eyes and one pair of ears could not keep account of them . . .

"A few minutes later the President of the Board of Trade, the Right Hon. William Graham, spoke into a microphone while cinematograph operators turned handles and photographers clicked shutters. He said: 'I have pleasure in declaring open this magnificent dock. It is at once a tribute to the enterprise of Messrs. Lever Brothers and to the development of this part of Merseyside and I wish it all possible success'. Then the photographers and cinematograph operators cheered in their turn; it was their field day; and the following Monday that message and those cheers were being reproduced in many cinemas throughout the country."

This transformation of one hundred acres of muddy foreshore and an insignificant stream into one of the largest private docks in the world was said to touch the well being of the entire British people. It had provided employment for 500 workers, increased Merseyside shipping facilities, and had brought Bromborough to the attention of new worldwide markets.

At the inaugural luncheon held in Hulme Hall young Lord Leverhulme spoke of his father's prudence regarding the great enterprise. "To find the origins of the present development at Bromborough we must go back to the year 1904, when my father purchased eight hundred acres of land along the shore of the River Mersey, thereby laying the foundations of what is now known as Bromborough Port" he said. "As the years go by the dock will become more and more a monument to the far-seeing vision of our late Chairman."

Mr. Graham responded with equal enthusiasm. The late Lord Leverhulme had not only given birth to a great company but had made a unique contribution to national and even international conditions of employment. He had made industry beautiful and dignified and had helped build a deeper and richer life for the thousands of workers who had been associated with him.

Twenty five years later the Port Sunlight News reflected upon the great enterprise. During the first year of working the wharves had handled 117,000 tons of cargoes while in 1955 over 685,000 tons were loaded and unloaded. This vast tonnage included the arrival of palm oil, kernels, copra and ground nuts from West Africa; timber from Scandinavia; tallow from the Great Lakes; whale oil from the Antarctic and molasses from the West Indies **and** Egypt; while outgoing cargoes included soap, margarine, cattlefoods and bulk oils.

In all the dock had built up an impressive record of achievement. This commemorative article concluded:

"George Saville, first Marquis of Halifax wrote: 'Wise Venturing is the most commendable part of human Prudence.' The First Lord Leverhulme, in looking at the foreshore of the Mersey between New Ferry and Eastham in 1904, planning for its future and beginning the dock in 1923, has been justified by history and has brought an aphorism to life."

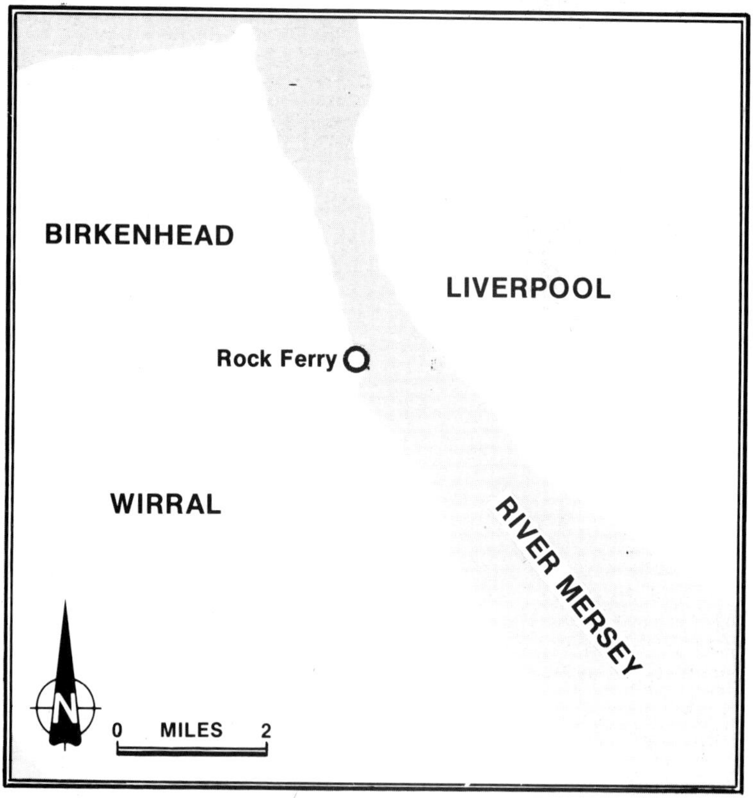

BIRKENHEAD

LIVERPOOL

Rock Ferry ⭕

WIRRAL

RIVER MERSEY

N

0   MILES   2

Chapter 4

WHERE THE NIGHTINGALE SANG

Rock Ferry.   Photograph: Harry Foster. Private Collection

The name Rock Ferry has a romantic ring.

To many people it evokes an image of clear waters and rocky shores; of an old raking slip-way and a busy landing stage; a clock tower gazing down from the roof of the ferry house towards crowded boats, perhaps from Eastham or Liverpool, that wait bobbing in the .river to tie in and set down their passengers.

In local diaries and archives there are probably more nostalgic glimpses of Rock Ferry than of almost anywhere else along the Wirral shores, which perhaps tells us something about the sheer extent of the decay that has crept along her streets and into her demeanour. For notwithstanding the renovation of many older properties and the creation of some areas of attractive new housing, Rock Ferry has become a dismal and unkempt place.

In numerous articles Bessie Cockburn, whose family lived in Peel Street, Tranmere, from 1911 to 1940, has written both vividly and poignantly about the area.

'A nightingale once sang here, it is said. As I surveyed the scene of what was once Rock Ferry pier it was like an old oil painting once beautiful but now daubed over in curves and circles with a white-wash brush.' Recalling the foreshore she says 'I could see children hanging over the sea wall watching conger eels swimming around, hoping to catch one with their hands. Alas, they were faster than the young fishermen.' There was 'nice yellow sand and even bathing huts' at the foot of St. Paul's Road. She remembers that 'echoes of the H.M.S. *Conway's* bells would carry across the water to people sitting on the promenade wall enjoying the sunshine on summer days and we would watch the cadets, or 'chums', coming over on the liberty boat with sports gear and running up the slipway to go to their sportsfield.

'Our tuck shop supplied the goodies for the boys coming and going to the ship, with a nearby small ships' chandlers where the tar smell was to me much finer than the costliest perfume.'

Nearby 'Mersey Road was a lane with fine houses and gardens . . . . (while) the old school at Parkton Grove was in an area of a handsome group of houses . . . . . Families, clad in cool summer dresses would sit gracefully in their gardens, the sounds of tennis racquets sharp in the mellow summer evenings, teas on the lawn while watching the ships sailing up and down the busy Mersey. Parkton Grove was a very private place indeed.'*

Fish and fishing featured large in the tales of Rock Ferry. Phyllis Hope tells us about the fishmonger's that was later known as Shaw's in Bedford Road, and of an unusual delivery of fish to the *Conway*.

'Shaw's originally belonged to Mr. Buchanan. James Buchanan was a Scottish sailor who often put into Park Gate. The story is told of the day he swam in the terrible Bay of Biscay with a rope between his teeth to save the life of a captain from Rock Park. As a reward the young sailor was set up in the fish business in Bedford Road . . . . He spent most of his working life sailing a fishing boat in the Mersey and supplying the shop which was run by his wife and daughter, Janie.'

'Janie Buchanan, with heavy baskets of fresh fish roped across her shoulders, stumbled across the uneven ice towards the *Conway* . . . . It was the fourth or fifth day of the freeze and there were lots of people walking out as far as the old ships . . . . With a good deal of huffing and puffing the baskets were hoisted up to the rail midships

---

*The Romance of Rock Ferry
(Birkenhead History Society Newsletter)

and emptied unceremoniously into waiting barrels. Money was lowered over the side together with a bundle of collars (?) to be washed, buckles to be polished and socks to be darned. The young cadets called (as much as they dared) their appreciation of the fish girl. 'Old Buchanan' watched from the stone slipway, disapproving of the excited reaction to his daughter, disapproving of the freezing weather, disapproving of everything except the money bags. He wanted to be busy. He usually fished as far out as the bar, but there would be no more catches that week: his boat was practically frozen to the slip.'*

Another reflection upon boats and shops appears in 'Bygone Birkenhead' by J.R. Kaighin.

'On that long stretch of muddy shore from Tranmere to Rock Ferry lay the *Akbar*, the *Indefatigable* and that leviathan of those days, the *Great Eastern* with its six tall masts and five funnels. Captain Potter was for many years an officer on the *Conway*. At our shop he was a customer for a fine white cotton cord used for making the chain attachment for the knives those youths training for the sea carried.'

In 1847 William Mortimer described the area thus:

Near the Ferry at Rock Park 'all the buildings are of a superior description, standing either alone, or in detached clusters of not more than three or four, in gardens which comport with the general appearance of the Park, through which are several pleasing and sheltered drives. At the north east extremity of these grounds on a gentle acclivity overlooking the Park stands a new church dedicated to St. Peter on the Rock.

'The river from this part assumes the appearance of an inland lake, the outlet being entirely concealed by the projecting land of Birkenhead . . . . The church, houses and hotel appear flanked with rich woodland scenery, whilst the river . . . . contrasts beautifully with the scenery of the surrounding country.'

One hundred and thirty five years after Mortimer's paragraph, Frank Forsythe wrote to a cousin in Alberta, Canada. Apart from personal greetings and news items his letter contained the following passage about Rock Ferry:

*Phyllis Hope in a taped interview.

49

H.M.S. 'Conway' lying off Rock Ferry.
Photograph: Private Collection.

Above: Bedford Road, Rock Ferry, looking towards the river.
Photograph: Layfield's Library, Rock Ferry. Private Collection

An invitation to the 'Akbar's' Autumn prize giving.

The Committee request the pleasure of your Company at the Annual Distribution of Prizes on board the Training Ship "Akbar" on Friday the 15ᵈ September by the Right Honourable the Lord Mayor of Liverpool

The Cunard Tender "Skirmisher" will leave the South end of the Landing Stage at 2·15 p.m.

Boats will leave Rock Ferry at the same time

The shore at Rock Ferry, 1984. View from the esplanade.
Photograph: Maurice Hope

'I decided to have a day in Rock Ferry last Tuesday for old time's sake. What a shock! It was so run down I could have cried. On New Chester Road, towards Tranmere, Boots, Woodson's, Murray's, Miss Mitchell's post office and most of the houses have been flattened. On the riverside of the road there's a big new industrial estate . . . . Many of the remaining shops are boarded up although a few (like Wharton's in Bedford Road) have kept up appearances. The Presbyterian church (the one with the top knocked off the steeple) is a little factory. Heaven knows what Mr. Lewis would say! . . . . The Baptist chapel is still there, but St. Barnabus', and the big Catholic Convent chapel (on the corner of Highfield Road) have been demolished . . . . The Palace cinema (I can still see Miss Slack at the pay desk, and the queues nearly down to the bus stop) is a car showroom now . . . . And can you believe that young Dr. Leggatt has retired? . . . . I was surprised to notice that the station ticket office on the hill has been knocked down (although the station itself is still operating) . . . .

The lower part of Bedford Road has been cut off by the New Ferry bypass, and a concrete wall running along Mersey Road (and carving up Rock Park) bars the way — and the view — to the river. To get to the shore you've got to go up to what used to be the Park entrance and across a new bridge. Most of the houses are kept nice (especially around where George Eager used to live) but down by the shore everything, except the Admiral pub, looks shabby and neglected. The Royal Rock has disappeared and you can't see the boat yard for mesh fences and great oil tanks . . . . There are heaps of rubbish everywhere and the esplanade looks out over a wilderness of old bricks and tin cans, abandoned arm chairs and bicycle frames all covered in black slime.'

* * * * * * * *

It is not clear exactly when the ferry at the Rock was founded although there is a reference to a 'boatman of Bebington' in various accounts of the seventeenth century, a period when Rock Ferry formed part of the township of Higher Bebington. It is recorded that in the early years of the following century services were somewhat erratic and often depended upon the humour of the boatman. In 1709 Nicholas Blundell, Liverpool-bound, arrived at the Rock only to discover that 'the boat was gone', so, as was the custom, he 'got some smoke made' to attract the ferryman's attention. The ferryman, however, turned a blind eye to these urgent signals and it was a disgruntled Mr. Blundell who was compelled to ride on to the comparatively dependable boatman at Woodside.

Joseph White of Sutton, who purchased part of the township of Higher Bebington (including Rock Ferry), made efforts to expand the ferry service at the beginning of the nineteenth century. He gained 'legislation for improving the passage between the town of Liverpool and the Country of Cheshire', and in 1804 he made proposals to establish a *second* ferry to ply between the Rock and the house he had bought on the Toxteth shore. The plan was defeated by Liverpool Town Council, however, and Mr. White had to be content with developing the existing route. It was at about this time that the first Rock Hotel was built, together with some simple facilities for entertainment in its grounds.

Meanwhile, numerous small rowing and sailing boats, both registered and unregistered, continued to convey travellers across the estuary.

The skipper of one such craft, a certain Mr. Matthews (who was reputed to have 'the biggest hand and foot in Cheshire'), delivered an unusual passenger to the Rock Hotel one summer's night. Mr. A.H. Jones, for many years Chairman of the Bromborough Society, the boatman's great great grandson, continues the story:—

> 'After the party had disembarked Matthews discovered a goldtipped stick in the boat. He walked up to the hotel and asked to see the passenger who had left it. A finely dressed gentleman entered, thanked him for his honesty, and gave him the stick as a reward. We can perhaps imagine the ferryman's astonishment when he was informed that the gentleman was none other than the King — George IV. The gift was later stolen from a Liverpool coffee house, Matthews having been treated to a pot of drugged coffee .... It is thought that the Rock Hotel was known as the Royal Rock from that time.'

Though Mr. Jones cannot vouch for the unqualified accuracy of this account, and although the 'Royal' designation is more likely to have derived from the Royal Navy's loading of Canadian and American mails from the shore slip, it is nevertheless fascinating to speculate upon the nature of such a visit by a King. Perhaps it is a matter we should not ponder too deeply!

In the days of sail the Rock was sparsely populated and buildings of any note were few. One exception, however, was Derby House, a seat of the Minshull family and subsequently the home of the Oakshotts. Set in Derby Park, which stretched from Old Chester Road to Rock Lane, the house was purchased by Richard Watson Barton who, in 1841, donated the land upon which St.Peter's church was built. In due course the Derby estate was dissected, first by a railway and then by the new road from Chester, and in 1844, much of what remained was sold for building. The house itself passed into the possession of the Oakshott family towards the end of the nineteenth century but neither history nor architectural merit could prevent its summary demolition following the death of Florence Oakshott, its last occupant.

Derby House is occasionally confused with the Manor House which was in fact built on the site of the present Morecroft Road by Thomas Morecroft who had purchased the rights of ferry in 1820.

By 1820 a fleet of steam paddlers, open-decked and relentlessly windswept, had appeared at various ferry points along the river bank, and had already brought to some Wirral hamlets the boldest of Lancashire's new refugees. But the Rock remained untroubled by settlers, for the time at least, for although Mr. Morecroft improved the jetty he was unable to afford a steamer until twelve years later, when he bought the *Aimwell* from a Clyde company.

Although these modern paddle boats defeated the river's swift currents, conditions aboard were far from congenial. Their cramped underdeck cabins were stifling and oppressive, and although landing slipways had been remodelled to include convenient steps, the measure of the tide was so great that at low water dignified ladies in expensive dresses were sometimes borne ashore on the hardened backs of chuckling crewmen. Not until the 1860s with the introduction of deck saloons and of Wirral's floating stages, were the hardships of the journey relieved, and the range of tides conquered. Again Rock Ferry, whose own floating stage did not materalise until 1899, was politely behind the times.

In 1836, however, a group of businessmen purchased the Rock estate with a view to development. The formation of the Royal Rock Ferry Company and the subsequent far reaching activity changed the face of the entire area. Plans were drawn up by Jonathan Bennison for a residential park to follow the bank of the Mersey, south from the Rock to New Ferry. Inspired by the habits of Regency architects who often planted surburban villas in secluded settings preserving the natural rise and fall of the land and creating comfortable perspectives, the new park reflected these ideals in its winding paths, gentle hillocks, and in varied architectural styles. Edward Hubbard in a paper written for the Victorian Society, calls it 'picturesque, sylvan informality'. He cites John Nash and Decimus Burton as the leading exponents of the style and suggests that although the houses (except for two or three all completed by 1850) are generally pleasant 'Rock Park is notable for its overall planning rather than its individual buildings.'

A villa in Rock Park.   Photograph: Maurice Hope

The Rock Ferry entrance to Rock Park. The policeman's lodge is on the right.
                              Photograph: State Series Private Collection
The New Ferry entrance to Rock Park.
                              Photograph: Valentine's Private Collection

Every care was taken to create a pleasing atmosphere for residents. They would be protected from the outside world by a policeman appointed to deter intruders and to collect tolls for entry. (Until the 1970s a board stood at the lodge beside the gates disclosing the latest charges).

'Rock Park was looked upon as a kind of exclusive area, and there were, in fact, entrance lodges of Gothic design at each end to guard the place against types that cause vandalism in this modern world. In the lodges lived the wardens (who) wore sideburns, silk hats and frock coats,' wrote Edward Lavell in a retrospective article that appeared in the Birkenhead News in 1970.

Financed by the residents themselves St. Peter's Church was built on a rise nearby. It is notable for its unique blend of sensible proportions and eccentric ornamental details.

'We got into our new house in Rock Park yesterday' wrote Nathaniel Hawthorne, 'it is a stone edifice, like almost all the English houses, and handsome in its design.

'Rock Park, as the locality is called, is private property, and is now nearly covered with residences for private people, merchants and others of the upper middling class, the houses being mostly built, I suppose, on speculation, and let to those who occupy them.

'On either side there is thick shrubbery, with glimpses through it of the ornamental portals, or into the trim gardens . . . . affording reasonable breathing space. They are really an improvement on anything, save what the very rich can enjoy in America.'

The park's special tone was firmly established when Nathaniel Hawthorne wrote the above account in his diary of September 2, 1853, the day on which he moved into number 26 Rock Park. But despite the romantic impressions he gained of the 'noiseless streets' and pretty residences, 'the damp twilight of the north of England' was slow to capture his affection. Eventually, however, he grew to love the house and his neighbours. Hawthorne's novel, 'The Old Home', was inspired in part by his Merseyside interlude, and indeed, having returned to the United States he wrote from his sick bed 'if I could go to England I think the sea and the sight of the Old Home would set me right.'

Amongst Hawthorne's eminent visitors to number 26 was James Buchanan, minister to Great Britain (quite unrelated of course to the aforementioned James Buchanan, Scottish sailor). Mr. Buchanan, who became the 15th President of the United States, must have enjoyed a stroll through the lanes 'shadowy with shrubs' and along the elegant riverside esplanade that stretched to New Ferry and offered a unique sanctuary from clattering carriages and panting horses. Looking at Rock Ferry today it is not easy to imagine both English Kings and potential American presidents relaxing in such a setting.

Many of the Park's private gardens opened out onto this attractive promenade thus adding considerably to their charm.

'The stroll along the esplanade was delightful, especially on Sunday evening' reflects Caroline Green '. . . . . ladies with their husbands enjoying the view and taking the fresh air . . . . The children enjoyed making sand castles and, best of all, picking the 'quens', or sea snails, from under the stones, taking them home to be washed and boiled . . . . . ' Many would walk to New Ferry to enjoy a picnic at Shorefields or a band concert, while others would patronise the shops and bathouses at the Rock Ferry end of the esplanade. Hot baths still represented undreamed of luxury to many people.

The environs of Rock Park, however, constituted only one small part of the whole for Rock Ferry gradually developed into a sophisticated and bracing suburb with excellent leisure facilities, efficient communications and a large variety of good quality housing and shops. One could play croquet, badminton, bowls and tennis, and on Saturday and Sunday afternoons the woods and gardens echoed the well-mannered applause from nearby cricket greens. One of the favourite and most beautiful grounds was the Dell where it was said games were played in the 'best traditional manner.' Fred Hoblyn recalls his happy visits to the Royal Rock Ferry Cricket Club, and

The Dell, Rock Ferry.   Photograph: Harry Foster

especially one occasion 'when a six hit out of the ground into Mr. John's greenhouse was greeted with rapturous applause'. For those with an appetite for the chase a 'pack of beagles for the purpose of hunting hounds over the Hundred of Wirral' was formed by Christopher Rawson Junior, while those with a taste for nautical adventure could turn to the Royal Mersey Yacht Club, later distinguished by the patronage of Sir Thomas Lipton (whose devotion to sailing was so ardent that he made five attempts to secure the Americas Cup). Mrs. Jean Hocking fondly remembers her father supplying fruit and vegetables for the King's dinner at the Sailing Club.

'The King took some of my father's filberts back to the yacht saying they were the best he had ever tasted. Father's chest, I recall, swelled with pride.'

Before the Great War a craze for roller skating evidently swept the country. Rock Ferry was quick to recognise a demand for a roller rink, and as early as 1877 the Palace Rink was opened, on New Chester Road next to the Wesleyn Chapel, by the Rock Ferry Skating Rink Co. Ltd. The heyday of the Palace, however, came with its conversion into a cinema in the days before the War. Many elderly cinema-goers will remember Professor Percy de Haas whose astonishing pianoforte technique brought the flickering pictures to life. Indeed P.D. and Mrs. P.D., as they were known, were familiar figures in Rock Ferry, particularly along Highfield Road, until the 1970s.

Poised on the elevated site of the old Rock House, the Royal Rock Hotel was perhaps the finest of the new hotels to be built along the coast in response to the demands created by the coaching and ferry companies. Before 1836 there had been a hostelry of sorts on the site but the fever of development and speculative building affected the construction of a good-looking hotel with an imposing classical portico and charming wood-panelled rooms looking across sloping lawns and beds of geraniums towards the forest of ships' masts clustered around Liverpool's Pier Head two miles downstream.

The new Royal Rock Hotel was completed in time to observe the final glories and subsequent decline in the exciting tradition of coaching, a tradition which had prospered on this very site for generations. The hotel's old stables and cobbled courtyards were acquainted with all the rush and bustle surrounding the very best coaches of the day. Well known local historian Harry Foster has made an intensive study of coaching. He maintains that the Royal Rock was the home of the celebrated 'Hibernia' whose epic race against its rival 'L' Hirondelle' from the Birkenhead Hotel in which 131 miles to Cheltenham were covered in an astonishing $9\frac{1}{2}$ hours was a classic of its age.

But in 1839, even as the new highways enhanced both coaching performances and Rock Ferry's accessibility, the ominous shadow of one George Stephenson loomed large. For some time the coach and ferry companies had been amassing evidence to forestall the inevitable challenge of the railways. In 1836, four years before the opening of Stephenson's Chester line, a census had been taken at the Sutton staging post. On that day, a Saturday in October, 49 coaches had passed through the Wirral post carrying 499 passengers. Impressive though such figures were, the gleaming new railway tracks were soon snorting with quite different noises and when the first locomotive, the 'Wirral', chugged out of Birkenhead, bound with its nine carriages for Chester's Brook Street, the fervent age of coaching was doomed. Eventually, despite the promise of new, better coaches, of improved staging posts, and despite even a programme of publicity stunts such as the famous coach versus train races, even the die-hards were forced to accept that progress could not be halted.

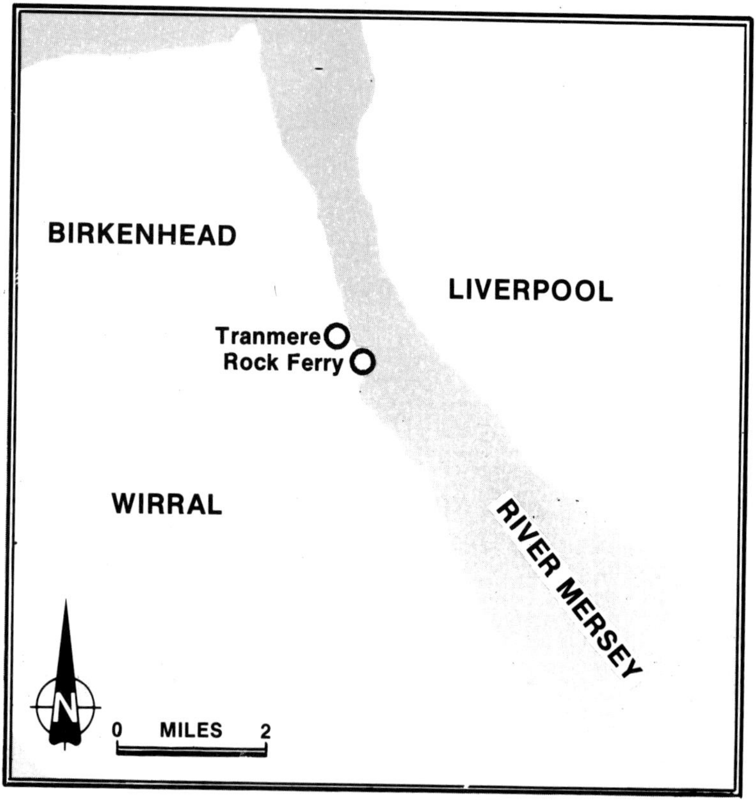

BIRKENHEAD

LIVERPOOL

Tranmere O
Rock Ferry O

WIRRAL

RIVER MERSEY

N

0   MILES   2

Chapter 5

BETWEEN TODAY AND YESTERDAY

The ferry services from the Rock continued to profit or decline according to the varying abilities and fortunes of the proprietors and the effects of changing external circumstances. In 1836, with the establishment of the Royal Rock Ferry Steam Packet Company, the iron paddle steamer *Alexander*, bearing a star at her mast top and advertised as 'the swiftest and best tow-er in the River Mersey', was placed on the crossing to Liverpool. For the next few years a succession of lessees — the Crippins, the Forsters, the Hetheringtons — took over ferrying responsibilities from the owners and introduced a number of interesting boats to the Rock Ferry jetty. There was *Cheshire Witch, Star, Sylph, Nymph, Ant* and *Bee* and, when the Steam Packet Company itself resumed liability, *Fairy Queen, Gipsey Queen*, and, in 1866, a second *Alexandra*. In 1877, the year in which Rock Ferry became part of the new County Borough of Birkenhead, the locally built *Queen of the Mersey* made a distinguished addition to the fleet. Twelve years later the ferry rights, boats, slipway and hotel were taken over by Robert Macfie, an experienced operator who had established a service from New Ferry, at the south end of the esplanade, in 1865. (A route which never really enjoyed total security but one which functioned under different managements until 1922). Mr Macfie was not notably successful at Rock Ferry and by 1892 the slipway was deserted.

Numerous appeals were made to Birkenhead Corporation to purchase the ferry but Mr. Macfie's trustees were reluctant to sell the Rock, unless, that is, the Corporation could be persuaded to buy the New Ferry as well. Negotiations persisted for 5 years and at last, late in the '90s, Rock Ferry was reopened with a new pier, a new steamer, *Firefly*, and a *triangular* service from New Ferry to Rock Ferry and Liverpool. The sister ships *Wirral* and *Mersey*, the first twin screw as opposed to paddle steamers, were brought into service at this time, and business was so good that the management introduced calls to Eastham in 1901.

A more human side of ferrying is picked up by Mr. Lavell in his 'Birkenhead News' article.

'Passengers were very different from those who throng the modern buses' he writes. 'Most men wore a gardenia or rose button hole, pearl pins in their ties and the usual gold hunter pocket watch.

'They wore a dark jacket and grey striped trousers, and businessmen sported frock coats and silk hats. The ladies in the summer wore picture hats and long white gloves, and they frequently carried parasols of shot-coloured silk.

'The engines of the ferry boats were visible through glass hatches, and it was great fun for the children to stand near the glass and watch the big piston rods move up and down.'

* * * * * * * *

Despite improved roads, a network of trams and even an electrified under river railway, the ferries chugged on.

Meanwhile, business and pleasure mingled on the beaches. For, as children jostled for their donkey rides and adults sampled their summer picnics, the Tranmere and New Ferry foreshores echoed with the tasks of ship-breaking.

Although many illustrious ships were dismantled on the flats, perhaps the most poignant episode was the interminable destruction of the 'grandest ship ever to sail the seas' — Brunel's folly, the *Great Eastern*. Entering the Mersey daubed with unbecoming advertising slogans for a Liverpool store, she was laboriously towed to her resting place in 1888 to be stripped and auctioned in 897 lots. Though the sale was successful enough (there are a few mementoes — some woodwork and glass screens — at the Great Eastern Hotel, New Ferry) demolition was a different matter. Built to ride the highest seas she was certainly not going to surrender to a few sledge hammers and crowbars. Finally, however, after a year's work, a deafening steam hammer was brought to the scene and in 1890, with the hull's resistance broken, a semblance of peace was restored to the shore.

Recollections of the river tend to be romantic and idyllic but some tell a different story. Mr. Hoblyn writes:

> 'I recall coming down to breakfast one January morning and my father telling my brother and me that he had been out half the night on receiving a telephone call from the staff at New Ferry pier that the *Mauretania* had broken adrift in the gale from her buoy in the Sloyne, the stretch of river off the Tranmere shore now partly covered by Cammel Laird's developments. As a Cunard official he was involved since it was feared she might collide with one of the . . . . training ships as she drifted. Somehow or other she missed these, passing *between Indefatigable* and the pontoon at the end of New Ferry pier and piling herself up on the shore at Garston where she remained for about a fortnight.'

Back in 1864 and again in 1899 local ferry boats were involved in daring offshore rescues. The first drama involved the *Lottie Sleigh* loaded with tons of dynamite and moored in the Sloyne. A flame from an overturned lamp was fanned towards the cargo and a sheet of fire shot into the sky. The Rock Ferry steamer *Wasp* pulled alongside and, at great risk, took off the crew. A few moments after her withdrawal the stricken ships was 'riven into a thousand pieces' in the biggest explosion Merseyside had ever known. *Wasp* was unharmed but there was widespread panic and damage to buildings and property on both banks of the river. The second *Conway* moored as she was little more than a mile away from the unlucky vessel did not escape unscathed.

. The 1899 rescue involved the *Clarence*, a reformatory ship for young offenders. Suddenly one night she caught fire and broke towards the shore. The ferry boats *Mersey* and *Firefly* plunged headlong into the flames, believed to have been started by the lads themselves, and carried both the officers and the boys to safety. By this time the *Clarence*, drifting helplessly, was a serious hazard in a crowded and confined river. A fire tender from the *Conway* was beaten back by the blaze so a gunboat was called. It apparently performed its duty with great skill and soon the old reformatory was only a memory.

The *Conways* themselves were perhaps the best known and almost certainly, to the residents of Rock Ferry, the best loved of the Mersey ships.

Over the years three *Conways* were moored in the river where the deeply guttered mud dipped beneath the low water mark. They shared the waters with a changing pattern of companions including an untidy group of lazarettos (or quarantine ships), and such handsome individuals as *Akbar*, *Nebar* and *Indefatigable*.

Mr. J.W. Gray's article on the subject of the three *Conways* is both interesting and informative.*

In the middle of the nineteenth century the Mercantile Services Association had been considering for some years the acquisition of a ship to serve as a floating base for the training of merchant navy officers. The first *Conway*, built at Chatham in 1828 was duly released by the Admiralty and brought to the Mersey during the winter of 1859. One hundred cadets had been enrolled in less than a year and soon a hospital, (Conway House), and the sports field in Knowsley Road had been purchased for their use. Within three years it became clear that the old ship was inadequate in size for the tasks placed before it. A second *Conway* (originally named the H.M.S. *Winchester*) arrived in 1862 and held her Mersey station for 14 years.

'One Conway II cadet of the mid-sixties 'reports Mr. Gray' was Matthew Webb who was to achieve fame in 1875 as Captain Webb when at the age of twenty seven he

*written for the Birkenhead History Society newsletter.

became the first man to swim the Channel, sadly to be drowned only eight years later in attempting to swim the treacherous Niagra Lower River.'

By 1876 a still larger ship was required. Accordingly H.M.S. *Nile* (*Conway III*) was provided by the Devonport authorities. Among H.M.S. *Conway's* smart cadets was John Masefield who, at the age of thirteen, joined the ship in 1891. In his biography, 'New Chum', published many years later, he nostalgically recalled his 'cramped life between decks', the smell of paint, the rush, tumult and order.'

'The *Conway* confidently entered the twentieth century, having by then passed out her 3000th cadet. Successfully weathering the First World War, she continued her great work as 'England's Floating Public School' right through the '20s and '30s.

'This third ship is the *Conway* still remembered by older people today. How splendid she looked when dressed overall on festive occasions such as Royal or Fleet visits to Merseyside, parents' days, prizegiving days and regattas . . . .

'How continually busy her boats and launches were, besides carrying boys, staff and visitors to Rock Ferry slip, transporting the mass of stores, laundry, coal and even fresh water from the shore!'

Many of the older residents of Rock Ferry have personal memories of the *Conway*.

'Speech days . . . . were great occasions', says Mr. Lavell, 'Rock Ferry guests would board by tender from the Liverpool landing stage. A complimentary speech would be made by Lord Lathom or Lord Derby.

'Tea would be served', writes Jean Hocking (Cheshire Life, March 1977) 'and the guests would admire the banks of flowers on the ships and multi coloured Chinese lanterns that were lit up when darkness fell.'

'We used to go to the Captain's quarters, and very splendid they were. At that time roller skating was all the rage and the cadets used to skate round the upper deck and come rushing up to us, only to do a quick turn just as we thought we were going to be swept off our feet in a very literal sense.'

'When my brother and I were children, we were once taken on board ship in the school holidays, as a great treat. I remember going down the stone slip at the side of

Rock Ferry Pier, and being helped into a motor boat, while it was rocking. Then, when all were aboard, off we went, with one of the men in charge of the small boat. It was strange and so different from being on a Ferry Boat! When the motor boat drew aside the *Conway*, we were helped aboard. We were actually *on* the ship we had often seen anchored in the Mersey! We saw where the boys slept, ate and worked, and the classroom. I remember their hammocks , and was impressed by hard sailor biscuits. It was a memorable day!'
Dorothy Harden. Birkenhead History Society Newsletter
March 19, 1979

In the opening years of the twentieth century Rock Ferry with her cultivated blend of old and new, of work and play, of rich and poor, was at the pinnacle of her career. One could mingle casually with the wealthy or rub shoulders with old soldiers and fishermen who could tell a story or two. The seasons were vital and stylish. Cavendish and Egerton Parks provided additional residences for affluent businessmen, while the more modest streets, where houses were usually arranged in neat terraces, were bright with floral baskets and climbing roses. Shopkeepers cared for the windows, pavements were regularly brushed, and paintwork was clean and colourful. The participation of all kinds of people in the activities of Rock Ferry appears to have been one of her happiest features. For Rock Ferry, despite her mansions and private boulevards, her titled visitors and officers in silver-laced blue uniforms with snow white gloves, never really became pretentious. Or if she did, she seemed prepared to abdicate her privilege of exclusiveness in the interests of courtesy and well-being. Snobbishness there must surely have been, but it did not obtrude in the manner of some other suburbs.

Apart from all of the opportunities offered by the *Conway* there seemed to be many other celebrations in Rock Ferry in those palmy days. Indeed many would suggest that Rock Ferry herself was the chief cause for rejoicing.

Although by the '20s a number of older families had forsaken the Rock to settle a little deeper in Wirral's unspoilt countryside, their departure made little immediate impact. The streets, the parks and the Ferry were still rich in characters and brisk with movement. Local fisherman continued to trundle their catches of lobsters, crabs and shrimps up the slipway to the crenellated gate-house, and you could still buy a bucket of fluke for a shilling! Evenings shone with lights from the Rock Vaults and from the Admiral public house where Bill Dunwin was a popular landlord for many years; and there was always bustle from Sam Bond's unsleeping boat yard.

Regatta days were still celebrated with flying flags and with children's competitions, and crowds lined the embankments to catch sight of the racing yachts. The townspeople of Liverpool still made it a very special treat to cross the estuary for afternoon teas in the gardens of the Royal Rock. On important occasions there were illuminated tram cars and spectacular visits from the Channel fleet.

At the Olympia Gardens sophisticated entertainments — often publicised by a couple of quite *unsophisticated* clowns, Tobo and Willy the One Man Band — vied with troupes of pierrots (perhaps the Cabaret Kittens or the Cigarettes) introduced by a Mr. Boult, the brother of Sir Adrian, for those with simpler tastes. And occasionally a 'Night of Stars' presented the truly Olympian delights of Wee Mona, Leslie Henson, Florrie Ford or Tommy Handley.

Nevertheless, the migration of the older families, the conversion of some of their villas into flats, and the attention of the new property developers who carelessly crowded poorly built houses into the nearest convenient spaces, began to sow the seeds of decline. The ferries, too, were in troubled waters. In 1922 New Ferry pier was rammed by a Dutch cargo ship and the cost of repairs to the stage and its connecting bridge was deemed to be too high to be economically feasible and so the service, though not officially discontinued until 1924 was actually abandoned there and then.

In the 1930s the electrified railway to Liverpool, and the Mersey road tunnel, *Queensway*, (opened in July 1934), finally caught up

The last days of the 'Conway'. Menai Straits, 1951.
Photograph: Private Collection

with the services from the Rock. Passenger traffic diminished, maintenance became increasingly expensive, and the Council found it necessary to recommend closure. On Friday, June 30th, 1939, the last boat pulled out. Many properties began to fall into disrepair, the beagles fled to Ledsham, the Olympia locked her gates, and, when the Second World War began the *Conway* was towed away to Anglesey. (Indeed it was in the Menai Straits, twelve years later, that the *Conway* finally met her Waterloo. As she was being towed back to the Mersey for a complete refit she broke loose, foundered on the banks and broke her back.)

In the meantime, the shops where rich patrons had once browsed — Austin's the outfitters, Holland's the jewellers, Ryalls and Jones' the music shop — and the long established family businesses — Vitty's the greengrocers, Manning's the confectioners, Tommy Hancock the butcher — had all but vanished, and the new tradespeople, feeling little affection for Rock Ferry, seemed to take a less personal interest in their customers and properties; while Houldin's shire-drawn coal wagons, clopping along Railway Road and rattling down Corinthian Street, were the only tangible link with the horse drawn hansons, landaus and Victorias that had once stood in neat ranks on the hill to the station.

The second war rumbled to a standstill, and after the weary thanksgiving Rock Ferry stumbled into a cloud of suspense. Her riverside situation was noted by hungry industrial eyes and plans were made to recover Tranmere beach in order to establish a colony of oil storage tanks. The pier was practically demolished and a long jetty was erected on its site, its far end branching into two huge bays where tankers could be pumped and flushed out before returning to sea. A metallic network of industrial installations crept towards the Royal Rock Hotel which held on until no more patrons came.

Perhaps worst of all — for the project appeared to have neither rhyme nor reason — a new by-pass threatened to dissect Rock Park. Objections were heard, registered, over-ruled and heard again.

What was so offensive about the plan was that, as Edward Hubbard pointed out, 'a practical alternative route exists for the road, and the unnecessary and shortsighted destruction of Rock Park is an unforgivable act of vandalism!'

The residents, like Rock Ferry itself, were caught between today and yesterday and did not know which way to turn. Finally, in 1975, European Architectural Heritage Year, the new road forced its way through the drawing room of Hawthorne house and surged past the heap of rubble once known as the Royal Rock Hotel.

Isolated figures still wander along the esplanade and some of the park's villas retain an air of make believe splendour but the river has become old and ugly and it no longer subscribes to the settlement it

Tranmere Oil Terminal from the shore, Rock Ferry.
Photograph: Alison Groves

nourished. Embarrassed, the people and the water pass each other by. What the Birkenhead News described, in 1970, as 'an air of drabness and depression overhanging the entire area', deepened in the following decade and spread into Rock Ferry's quietest recesses where, it was said, the nightingale once sang.

* * * * * * * *

Shipbuilding and various other maritime interests occupy the river bank from Rock Ferry to Woodside. Along what used to be the Tranmere foreshore the old ferry has disappeared, together with Gonnell's Pool and Birket (or Tranmere) Pool, beneath the area which has been reclaimed from the river. Close to the water the low lands are flat and featureless, the railway and the road cutting through them like a furrow and fold. By contrast the small township of Tranmere itself sits on a high, steep ridge, a thousand yards or more back from the shore. Barred by shipyards and oil tanks she enjoys no immediate access to the river. Indeed Tranmere is a victim of one of Birkenhead's most peculiar and most infuriating habits — a tendency to build high walls and fences which effectively seal off the estuary from the town and its inhabitants.

Yet there was a time when this was a particularly lively part of the coast. Offshore the Sloyne was reputedly the safest anchorage in the

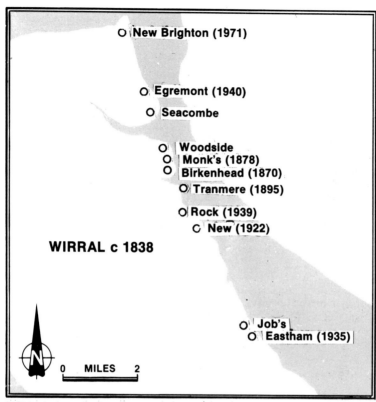

O New Brighton (1971)

O Egremont (1940)

O Seacombe

O Woodside
O Monk's (1878)
O Birkenhead (1870)
O Tranmere (1895)

O Rock (1939)
C New (1922)

WIRRAL c 1838

O Job's
O Eastham (1935)

N

0   MILES   2

WIRRAL ferry landings with dates of closure where appropriate.

Mersey, and day and night the commotion of mooring boats and of transporting crews to and from the waterfront kept the area busy. The beach too was seldom silent. It was a veritable adventure playground for the young, and many a local lad learned to swim in the deep and dangerous gutters that crossed the flats, while the railings that marked the boundary of Cammel Laird's 'shippy' made exciting climbing frames for the children who cartwheeled and tightroped their way to the water. Bessie Cockburn tells of the games she and her friends played in the boats that lay ready for breaking on the shore. There were many gory battles between pirates and crews, battles that were fought out to the last man, especially in the school holidays. She recalls how they would tie long lines to punts and would float out into the current as long as their nerve held firm.

There was also a lot of activity away from the shore. A football ground for local teams skirted St. Paul's Road.

'We would go there on Saturday afternoons' Mrs. Cockburn reports, 'to watch the Skins, a team from the Leather Works, or the Suds, the Port Sunlight team . . . . A field with Warren's cottages graced the side of the shipyard. I think they had a nursery and sold plants . . . . Each year a fair came as an added attraction for the local kids . . . . There were allotments for many years right down to the shore, and I remember men playing with Crown and Anchor boards, gambling until the police made one of their periodic raids . . . .'

For many years the nearby coastline tolerated the toils and troubles of several ferry companies. In addition to Tranmere itself, Birkenhead Ferry was situated just across the Pool. Tranmere Ferry and Birkenhead, which boasted a lovely hotel and 'extensive pleasure gardens backed with a belt of old oak trees,' operated as one company for some periods in the nineteenth century, for they were acutely aware of the advantages enjoyed by the rival service at Woodside, 'the safest and shortest passage across the Mersey', which stood beyond a small headland a little to the north of yet another crossing, Monks Ferry. Over the years an intense contest between these various concerns developed and any new ideas which seemed to offer an attractive advantage were eagerly accepted by the respective companies. In 1817, for example, the inauguration of steamer services from Tranmere gave her an important initiative. For a time her proud advertisements referred somewhat scathingly to the

Woodside Ferry, 1791.   Private Collection

70

'common sail boats' of Woodside. Yet with the intensification of the steam race Tranmere's own innovatory steamer, *Etna*, became only one amongst many paddle boats scurrying across the Mersey. Soon Birkenhead Ferry (under the auspices of La French and Company who already controlled Tranmere) followed suit with *Abbey* and *Vesuvius*, while Woodside (strongly motivated by innkeeper and ferry proprietor, Hugh Williams) responded to the challenge with the introduction of the *Countess of Bridgewater* and the brand new *Royal Mail*.

As the century proceeded, however, a number of factors united to confirm the pre-eminence of Woodside as a ferry terminus, and despite the linking together of Tranmere and Birkenhead in 1852 by the erection of a long wooden bridge across the Pool, the latter was eventually overwhelmed by the extension to Laird's shipyard, while the former, notwithstanding the opening of a new pier in 1877, fell prey to her own geographical position a quarter of a mile from the river's edge at low water. At the turn of the century the hectic contest was abandoned.

Monks Ferry, though comparatively short-lived, had a more controversial career than most.

Based at Ivy Rock, round the corner of the headland, she somewhat brazenly joined the steamer race in 1835. Woodside, evidently displeased by an additional source of competition, lodged an immediate complaint to the effect that the company held no legal right to operate their chosen route. Unmoved, the newcomer responded that the crossing actually constituted a revival of the ancient route of the monks. Since Woodside herself was, at least geographically, a more likely successor to the monks, such a defence was implausible and the Monks Ferry Company was forced to cease operations. But in 1840, with the arrival of the Chester-Birkenhead Railway, the pendulum swung again. With the completion of the line it was decided that Grange Lane Station, the elected terminus, was so inaccessible as far as the ferries were concerned, that a rail extension should be built to the handiest crossing point — Ivy Rock! In consequence by 1845 Monks Ferry had quickly re-established herself, and had become an important boat-train terminus. The glory, however, was shortlived for the Commissioners for the Improvement of Birkenhead threw their considerable weight behind Woodside whose advantages included a large and esteemed hotel (for many years a major coaching station with stabling for one hundred horses), a supreme position on the north corner of the headland, and a spacious concourse fit for modern development. Despite some moments of inefficiency and even mismanagement Woodside prospered. In due course such trusted boats as *Frances, Hercules, Eliza Price* and *Tobermory*, wooden to the core, were replaced by *Prince*, and *Queen*, two of Laird's *iron* ships; landing places were

71

improved, slipways were widened, while a long skilfully constructed dividing wall sheltered passengers and boats from almost any prevailing wind. A new landing stage was built, gas lamps were set up, a jointed floating road was constructed, and a fleet of gauche luggage boats took to the water. (This lucrative service for both vehicles and goods of every description produced a number of unusual craft which were only supplanted in the 1930s with the opening of Queensway Tunnel).

In view of the comprehensive nature of Woodside's services and facilities the Railway Companies abandoned Monks Ferry in 1878, and extended their line to an impressive new mainline terminal at Woodside itself.

The Queensway Road Tunnel.
Photographs: Dennis and Sons Ltd. Private Collection

The floating stage, Woodside.
Photograph: The Wrench Series. Private Collection

Woodside Ferry in the 1950s.
Photograph: Dennis and Sons Ltd. Private Collection

The next two pages show photographs of Woodside Ferry Terminus.

73

Photographs:
Maurice Hope

Photographs:
Maurice Hope

BIRKENHEAD
The Headland O

LIVERPOOL

WIRRAL

RIVER MERSEY

0   MILES   2

Chapter 6

LITTLE HEADLAND OF BIRCHES

The little headland of birches rises from the river to the north of Tranmere pool just beyond the deep-cut graving docks and shipyards. In days gone by it was an isolated spot. Standing well away from the established tracks and beyond a tidal inlet it was awkward to reach. In fact even today — though for different reasons — reaching the headland can be a somewhat frustrating exercise, for the modern flying carriageway supporting a tangle of trunkroads neatly bypass the area, and either plunge the would be visitor into the depths of the Mersey Tunnel, or whisk him away past the gasworks towards the town centre. If the approach is confusing, however, arrival itself might at first glance be no more rewarding. For here the great walls of Birkenhead, occasionally spiked with splintered glass, truly come into their own. In preserving industrial security the walls often destroy the spectator's perspectives in a series of blind alleys. As for the buildings and streets, they give one an uneasy feeling, suggesting as some of them do, a reversal of nature: for while temporary structures have somehow acquired an aura of permanence natural features almost seem to intrude. Industrial premises impose their right of occupation and it is easy to assume that the towering banks of floodlights and straining gantries have defined the landscape's profile since the beginning of time. In these surroundings red soils and sandstone outcrops appear as impositions upon the natural order of things, and nothing seems less convincing than coarse grasses and dandelions toiling through the gravel of disused goodsyards, or stunted trees loitering uncomfortably in specially designed retangles of soil, like exhibits from another world. Nature hangs upside down on the headland of birches and it seems ironic that an environment so totally man-made should offer so little hospitality to man himself.

Yet there are other faces to this little headland. Castle Street and Church Street are typified by neat rows of houses; in Pilgrim Street (where incidentally Lord Birkenhead was born in 1872) the playground of Gillbrook School is often a blur of darting children; while closely by stand the handsome premises of Perry's the Sailmakers, a building which was originally the hotel for Monk's Ferry Railway Station.

St. Mary's Church, whose 130 feet spire dominates the headland, stands high above the river. Once surrounded by meadows and pleasant woodland St. Mary's, the first parish church of Birkenhead, is a monument to an age when certain privileged men possessed both the will and the means to develop unspoilt areas as resorts for gracious living. They would build hotels and mansions and churches to feed and sustain body and soul, they would promote efficient modes of transport, and their efforts would make them content and wealthy. Francis Price, the owner of the headland, embarked upon such a course in about 1815. Four years after the establishment of a residential locality he determined to enhance the area by commissioning a church from Thomas Rickman. Further, he resolved to have the building constructed entirely at his own expense. On July 19th, 1819, the foundation stone was laid, and in 1822 the church, with Gothic pinnacles and battlements (and stocks set in the churchyard wall), was consecrated by the Bishop of Chester. There was to be a peal of six 'fine-toned bells', and a tower furnished with a large clock ('placed much too low for general utility' as Mortimer complained some years later).

By the 1970s the church was riddled with dry rot. The authorities conferred and decided that it should be demolished. Such a conspicuous landmark, however, had powerful allies and, as a result of further discussions, complete demolition was averted. Instead a somewhat eccentric compromise was adopted: the bulk of the building was to be dismantled while the wall that looked along St. Mary' Gate towards Chester Street and New Chester Road, together with the fabled spire itself, were to be retained. This plan having been executed, the remains of St. Mary's today look like an elaborate film set - two dimensional, and rather comic.

The remains of St. Mary's church still dominates the headland.
Photograph: Maurice Hope

A quiet corner in the grounds of the Priory. Photograph: Alison Groves

The Norman chapel. Photograph: Private Collection

The tomb of the Lairds overlooks their shipyard from the cloisters of the Priory.
Photograph: Alison Groves

The most interesting feature of the headland, however, is neither her industrial creations, nor even St. Mary' Church. What then, could possibly attract the visitor to this fairly unprepossessing backwater? All around there are clues. We have already noted Pilgrim Street and Monk's Ferry. We could also have picked out Abbey, Abbot and Prior Streets, or perhaps the large notice board that reads PRIORY INDUSTRIAL ESTATE. For here, wedged tightly between Graving Dock number 5 and the Lighting Centre lie the ruins of the Priory of St. James the Great, the cradle of Birkenhead itself.

Even in today's dissonant surroundings the tiny Benedictine Priory may still evoke a moment or two of tranquility. Indifferent towards spectacular effect its import lies in an almost palpable modesty. The twelfth century chapter house, vaulted and stone-groined with simple ribs, is the only complete Norman building in Wirral. Having been regularly used for centuries as a chapel it has a very strong lived-in feel, and its windows reflect a secure, warm light. Though scholars have continually argued about the function of the room above the chapel, it is usually referred to as the Scriptorium. Whatever its use it displays fine panelling and a handsome timber roof. The intimate space of the cloister, around which the remaining buildings are grouped, was converted into a burial ground in the nineteenth century. Many tombs were crowded into this small quadrangle and of those that remain one especially worthy of attention is that of the Laird family, the effective founders of modern Birkenhead. Alongside the cloisters stand the remains of the great hall, where important guests would dine and perhaps await a

A nineteenth century study of the Priory.   Private Collection

81

propitious tide. Below lies the sombre fourteenth century crypt where the lesser guests supped and wined. Here the columns appear to grow from the red sandstone bedrock with an inevitability that perpetuates the landscape itself.

In his book 'Birkenhead Priory and After', Mr. W.F. Bushel, evokes a picture of the area where the Priory was built:

> 'Now consider the spot that was chosen' he writes. 'It must have been a striking headland, surrounded on three sides by water. On the south was a creek, Tranmere Pool, full of water at high tide, going up via the Gas Works of today nearly to Central Station . . . . . Then on the north the Wallasey Pool was a mile wide and the water was far nearer than it is now . . . . . Surely it was a beautiful site. Look at it with the eyes of eight centuries ago, not with the eyes of today!'

William Mortimer (admittedly not with the eyes of eight centuries since, but with the eyes of 1847) describes the significance of the buildings as follows:

> They are, he claims, 'the only remains in this neighbourhood of any importance, nor are there of equal antiquity on the opposite coast of Lancashire; their character is attested by every writer on the subject. . . . .
>
> 'It is greatly to be desired that measures may be adopted to prevent their falling into utter and oblivious decay.'

In view of this eloquent appeal and of the considerable merit of the buildings, one is bound to ask how has Birkenhead treated its distinguished inheritance. The answer is until recent years not very well! One feels that the Priory should have transcended political and economic wrangles, particularly as it exists in a corner of England not overendowed with examples of ancient architecture; that such a building should have been regarded as the glory of the headland, and should not have had to fight for its very existence; that it should have been considered as something other than a thorn in the side of commercial and industrial developers.

Yet on the other hand one might argue that the Priory has been fortunate to have survived at all in an area so comprehensively sacked by industry; and possibly it is not surprising that, in the face of commercial debates and struggles for improved ship building and docking facilities, it should have been regarded as somewhat mischievous and dispensable intruder.

The Priory of St. James enjoyed some four hundred years of prosperity before Henry VIII demanded its dissolution and forced its inmates to disperse. As a result many of its buildings were destroyed, some were used as dwellings or barns, while others gradually fell into disuse. A sequence of drawings and watercolours, the best of which (those by William Herdman) form part of an excellent collection in the Williamson Gallery, show the priory in ever advancing stages of decay, its walls crumbling, its foliage growing wild and only its chapter house maintaining a semblance of order. Little or nothing was done to improve matters until 1896. It was in this year that Birkenhead Corporation set up a public subscription scheme to purchase for preservation those parts of the estate not protected by the Church of England. But although a number of restoration projects were put in hand the Priory's troubles were by no means over. Indeed perhaps the most dramatic challenge to its existence came not from the careless neglect of past centuries but from the industrial ambition of our own. When, in 1957, a new dock was begun adjacent to the estate excavation gnawed into the ancient churchyard and devoured the remnants of the thirteenth century nave. Mercifully, however, the heavy industrial tread was halted at the last possible moment, a few yards from the doorstep of the chapel itself. Even then fortunes were slow to improve and, despite floods of proposals, no satisfactory programme has emerged. In fact until quite recently, the buildings have remained secreted behind crooked railings and stout padlocks.

Yet historians and archaeologists have continued to be impressed. The Priory's social influence together with its day-to-day activities

Birkhedde Priory, Cheshire. Published 10 October, 1783 by S. Hooper.

have been recorded by numerous distinguished authors over many years. Scholarly concoctions of fact and informed conjecture by Mortimer, Stewart-Brown, Fergus Irvine and Bushel, by McIntyre and Allison (to mention but a few) have been reproduced or summarised in countless subsequent documents. Nevertheless it would be inappropriate, even in the confines of the present brief chapter, to omit a story so crucial to the growth of Birkenhead. And so, with deference, we shall include an outline of events.

In about 1150 Baron Hamo de Masci from Dunham village granted part of his Wirral estate for the foundation of a Benedictine monastery. In due course a small band of black robed monks tramped from Chester to their wooded headland beside an estuary which had once served as the boundary between Mercia and Northumbria. Their path crossed a 'riverside meadow', a peninsula highlighted by ·sandstone ledges carved and piled like reluctant fortresses protecting woodland and dale. Although the Mersey tides were often savage and unpredictable — she was known as a 'wild beast of a river' — the monks could nonetheless be well pleased with their new home. On a coast indented with coves and bounded by heathland, its pools and streams teeming with salmon-trout and herring, the headland must have offered a setting as rich as anything England could boast.

The Benedictine order was well known for its temporal interests, and the Prior of Byrkenhed was empowered to 'hold a court in the Manor of Claughton'. He also held privileges for wreckage and fishing, and, exercising his manorial rights, would often ride to Bidston or Moreton to settle disputes on his lands. Further, he was wont to encounter the wrath of the Forester of Storeton whose strict enforcement of the forest law was less than applauded by the Benedictine residents. Long trips to Chester to plead against the Forester's charges became an almost habitual incident in the Prior's career. Such visits persisted until the Black Prince, who was then Earl of Chester, finally disafforested Wirral late in the fourteenth century. Hospitality, too, was among the responsibilities of the Prior and his band of brothers, and occasionally on stormy days the guests rooms at the Priory would be crowded with frustrated travellers and distracted monks.

It must have taken a stout courage to sail tiny boats across the broad river, but having mastered its moods, the brothers entered into fierce competition with Liverpool's wily boatman for freight and passengers. Across Tranmere Pool, where the monks probably moored their boats, a course of stepping stones was laid, and a path was fashioned from the Priory to its grange at Claughton, a path whose memory lingers in the name Grange Road.

Wordly though the Benedictines were, however, they were primarily 'Knights of Christ to whom the spiritual world was very real and very near.' Mr. J.E. Allison, local historian and scholar, unearthed some near-forgotten verses by a certain Reverend J. Keating which are worth recalling:*

The Chant of the Monks

The king hath Knights to fight his wars,
And guard his throne from scath and foe,
And warriors proudly bear the scars
That courage prove and duty show,
And love must always undergo.

God's Knights are we; no earthy sword,
We wear or wield, but bravely we
Do battle 'gainst the infernal horde,
As Christ's devoted chivalry,
To hold him for our souls in fee.

And there, where Mersey's waters meet
The waters of a silver main,
We launch abroad our peaceful fleet;
We ply the rod and cast the seine,
We win our bread with joy and pain.

For every blessing here below
Our grateful thanks we duly raise
To Him from whom all blessings flow,
Uplifting gladly, all our days,
A never-ending song of praise.

Birkenhead Priory was not conceived on the grand scale of a noble cathedral. Although it was no doubt considerably larger than the present remains would indicate the foundation never housed more than sixteen monks at any one time and was never elevated to the status of an abbey. The Priory expressed in simple terms the ideals of a working home, and yet it beheld some great occasions.

In the year 1201 King John served a writ for its protection while in 1275 and again in 1277 Edward I, the great mediaeval monarch, stayed there. His second visit lasting for five days attracted people from miles around eager to catch a glimpse of their imposing ruler and his knights and men-at-arms who spread a vast and colourful encampment across the headland. This formidable occasion is portrayed in three stained glass windows which may now be found in Birkenhead Town Hall, their mature colours faithfully recalling this moment of glory.

---

*Reproduced from The Liverpool Festival Song Book, 1907, in the Newsletter of the Birkenhead History Society.

E.W. Cox's impression of the Priory in its heydey.   Private Collection

In 1318, exhausted by the burdens of freely dispensed hospitality the Prior presented a petition to Edward II seeking permission to build separate lodging houses and to be permitted to sell refreshment to travellers. A Royal Charter granted the Prior's requests:

'— From the town of Liverpool . . . . . unto the Priory in the Country of Birkenhead,' read the letters patent, 'and from the same Priory unto the aforesaid Town beyond the arm of the sea there, a common passage is used, and on account of contrariety of weather and frequent storms, great numbers of persons wishing to cross there from the said Country of Chester into parts of the County of Lancaster, being often hindered, it hath hitherto been necessary to turn aside to the said Priory, by reason that at the passage aforesaid there are not any houses for lodging such persons; nor can any provisions be there found to be bought for the support of the said persons; on account whereof, the said Priory hath hitherto been burthened beyond its means, and the aforesaid persons have been very much wearied and grieved: WE, willing in this behalf to apply a remedy, of our special grace, have granted and given licence, for us and our heirs, as much as in us lies, to our beloved in Christ, the Prior and Convent of Birkened, at the place of the passage aforesaid, or as near as shall most conveniently be done, to build sufficient houses for lodging such persons; and the same being built may hold to them and their successors forever, and that the persons who shall dwell in the same houses may bring and sell provisions for the support of the men there, about to cross the said arm of the sea, without the hindrance or impediment of us or our heirs . . . . etc.'

It was not, however, until a further twelve years had elapsed that a second petition, this time to Edward III, granted the much more profitable rights of ferrying from Birkenhead to Liverpool (not, it should be noted, from Liverpool to Birkenhead, a distinction that occasionally caused some conflict of interests in later years). The second charter granted to the Prior and Convent

'a passage beyond the said arm of the sea, as well for men as for horses, and other things whatsoever; and for the same passage may receive as shall be deemed reasonable . . . . .'

This ferry charter — commemorated in the Lee tapestry at the Williamson Art Gallery — established the Mersey crossing as a bona fide business operation, one for which, incidentally, Birkenhead retained the financial monopoly until recent years (as the toll booths at Woodside testified).

It is interesting to note that even the original tolls, ranging from one farthing for a foot passenger (a toll doubled on market days) to one penny for a mounted man (or two pence if his horse were laden), were considered at the time to be 'excessive and exorbitant'.

In the fourteenth and fifteenth centuries the placid scene around the headland was but seldom disturbed. Once a ferryman was attacked and his passengers robbed by strangers from the woods; on another occasion someone made off with the Prior's boat in the middle of the night, but by and large farming and ferrying continued unhindered, religious offices went on uninterrupted and the monks kept up their various activities without a care for the passing years.

The continuity of nearly four hundred years of diligent civilization was rudely shattered by the dissolution of the monasteries in 1536. Birkenhead was left not only without a monastic settlement but without even the makings of a hamlet. Leland, who visited Wirral less than five years after the dissolution remarked 'hard on Wyral shore is Birket, late a priory, without any village by it.' In 1545, however, the headland and its properties, which had been retained by the Crown for almost a decade, were purchased by Ralph Worsley, a former page at the King's Court. Worsley acquired not only the Priory and its ground but 'the house, edifices, mills, barns, stables . . . . . one dove house . . . . . all the fish yards, and two acres of arable land where flax used to grow, and all the ferry, and the ferry-house, and the boat called *Feribot*, and the profit of the same.'

Naturally such properties and priviliges were not inexpensive, and Worsley's account came to £568-11s-6d.

Thomas Powell, who married Worsley's daughter, became lord of the manor in 1572. It was he who created, from a wing of the monastry, Birkenhead Hall, a pleasant house enjoying landscaped lawns, dotted with trees, gently sloping away to the red rocks of the shore. The old chapter house continued to serve as the manor's chapel. Despite a number of arguments relating to the ferries (Mr. Powell offended the authorities by carrying passengers *from* as well as *to* Liverpool) the quality of life was not unduly strained until 1643 when, as a token of general unrest, a body of Cavaliers 'kept guard about Berkett Wood . . . . and did shoote over the river to Liverpool towne'. Two years later a troop of Parliamentarians took possession of 'Berkett House in Worrall' and reduced some parts of it to ruins. But after the Civil War peace returned to the banks of the Mersey and the seasons passed with gentle indifference.

The estate's next master, John Cleveland, a prominent Lancashire merchant and member of parliament for Liverpool, improved the ferry services in a bid to encourage settlement, but even then his wary colleagues, suspicious of wind and tide, were not tempted to take up residence on the Cheshire side, and so, even at the close of the eighteenth century, Birkenhead, with a population of fewer than one hundred persons, remained a tiny hamlet 'disturbed neither by the Industrial Revolution nor by the growth of the City on the other side of the Estuary.'

Of the various factors that finally swept Birkenhead into the modern world the establishment of steam powered ferry boats and the ensuring revolution in communications was the most decisive. Yet even in this new age of powerful machines, an age when beaten tracks were swiftly abandoned and new courses were set, it was the handiwork of individuals that shaped the Merseyside of years to come. Men like William Laird who created a shipbuilding empire to challenge the world and who envisaged a city of wide boulevards and handsome public buildings. A glimpse of his splendid conception is provided by the facades of Hamilton Square, and it is unfortunate that the grandeur of his architectural plans (the realization of which he entrusted to Gillespie Graham of Edinburgh) should have remained unfulfilled. Only in his great ships were his dreams divulged.

By the middle of the nineteenth century Birkenhead had experienced a staggering transformation. She had endured both expansion and economic slump. She had factories, workshops, shipyards, elegant houses and shops, wide gas-lit streets (and

William Jackson's Gas Works to service them). She had a rail link to the far reaches of the country, a globe-lit market, a beautiful park designed by Joseph Paxton and a company of Commissioners to conduct the affairs of the population of nearly 25,000. Nationally and even internationally she had caused something of a stir. Indeed in 1845 a remarkable article appeared in Chambers Edinburgh Journal:

> 'Such is the hugeness of the power created by the industry and wealth of this country' it read 'there is at least one city which will undoubtedly have risen within the brief space between the boyhood and manhood of its first inhabitants. We allude to Birkenhead on the Mersey near Liverpool . . . . . It is one of the greatest wonders of the age and indeed one of those by which the character of our age is most strikingly expressed . . . . . Landing from one of the steamers, which cross the Mersey every half hour, we walked into this City of the Future with expectations which the reality by no means disappointed . . . . . we feel assured that, if the contemplated works shall be duly completed, the banks of the Mersey will present the grandest monument which the nineteenth century has erected to the genius of Commerce and Peace.'

Birkenhead Town Hall, Hamilton Square.
Photograph: Lewis's Series. Private Collection

89

In 1847 the Illustrated London News published a sonnet dedicated to the wonders of the new city, 'another glory on Mersey's side: a town springs up, as from a magic wand,' while in the same year Disraeli's 'Tancred' included a passage in which Birkenhead was compared with Damascus, 'a city full of life, wealth and enjoyment, a city always young and always rich'.

And yet in a hundred different ways the seeds of conflict were awaiting dispersal, for, as Professor Dore points out* initiative and vision were not in themselves enough, for ideas were frequently contradictory and almost from the outset Mr. Price, the Lairds and the Jacksons, were involved in incompatible schemes and even personal feuds: 'the atmosphere of a boom town did not favour consistent planning'.

In our next chapter we shall examine one of the great schemes, the construction of the dock estate, in a little detail. We shall meet again some of the city's founders and shall follow some of their strategies but we shall take care not be to tempted into an extensive history of Birkenhead. So far we have endeavoured (with varying degrees of success) to restrict ourselves to the changing scenes of the shoreline and in the present chapter our subject has been the little headland and, especially, the fortunes of the Priory.

Thinking again of the Priory is it any wonder that a town so volatile in its history should consider it superfluous? And yet again, noting the decay of some parts of the town, could it be that the Priory has unknowingly led a charmed life? Sacked by a King, domesticated by lords of the manor, bombarded by Cavaliers, defeated by vandals and nearly wiped out by industrialists, it has simply refused to perish. Services are still held in the Norman chapel and writers and scholars continue to be drawn to the stories that might even now be awaiting discovery. The gates are open to the public again, and although both the Church of England and the Wirral Authorities have extraordinary financial problems to solve, it appears that they are at least determined to display with pride what remains of the Priory of St. James the Great.

Indeed in the late summer of 1982 an imaginative plan for the foundation of a heritage park on the headland site was proposed by quantity surveyors James Nisbet and Partners, together with architects Kingham, Knight Associates. The so-called Monks Ferry Heritage Park immediately received the support of the Wirral Leisure Services Committee, the North Western Tourist Board, Merseyside County Council, the Birkenhead History Society and numerous other interested parties.

---

*'Cheshire' Batsford.

90

The scheme aims to transform the disused Ferry Brow, the abandoned graving docks of Western Ship Repairs, and the Priory itself into a park of rare historical distinction. A riverside walk, a maritime museum, picnic areas looking out across the estuary, and a deep sea aquarium, as well as 'high-quality' housing, are envisaged in a plan that could capitalize on the declining fortunes of recent years and could even reawaken a tired old waterfront.

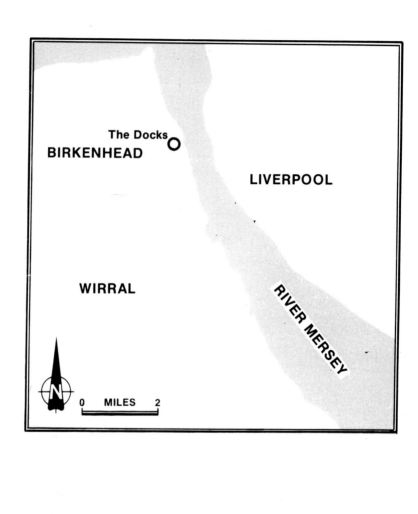

The Docks○
BIRKENHEAD

LIVERPOOL

WIRRAL

RIVER MERSEY

N

0   MILES   2

Chapter 7
A NEW CITY OF SHIPS

Today there is a certain greyness where the ports of Birkenhead and Liverpool come face to face. It would seem that, for the moment at least, ambition has fled, and that imagination, which so often dominated the growth of Birkenhead, has dried up. Across the almost unoccupied river the gaunt features of Liverpool docks stretch as far as the eye can see. Created from precisely arranged blocks of cyclopean granite the massive sea wall hides an empire of impounded docks vast enough, it would appear, to accommodate any number of ships.

By comparison the frontage of the Birkenhead dock estate is almost insignificant, for here the captive waters reach inland following the line of the creek called Wallasey Pool. Miles of quays and hundreds of acres of reclaimed land lie behind a half-mile river-facing dam, the very existence of which certifies a programme of dockland drama which was long and complicated. Its action was sporadic, its motives confused and its leading characters ranged from incompetent blunderers to men of skill and integrity. Finally the plot was animated by the divided interests of the Birkenhead waterfront, residential desirability, industrial settlement and political and commercial jealousies.

The old one o'clock gun.   Photograph: Dale Series. Private Collection.

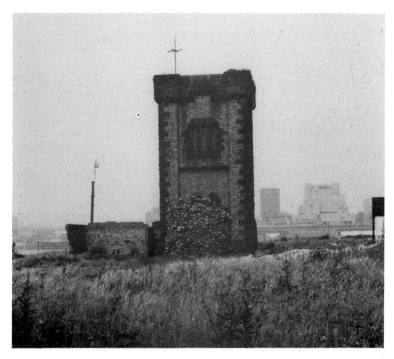

The accumulator tower, Birkenhead Docks.　　Photograph: Alison Groves

The closure of the Morpeth locks some years ago left only one entrance to the Birkenhead dock system from the river. Passing between the estuary and the Alfred Dock the twin branches* of this deep corridor are divided by a narrow wedge-shaped island bearing the lock keeper's cottage, tons of abandoned machinery, weathered iron castings and a sturdy wind-grained watchtower of stone and brick, a tower whose true function — to house a powerful accumulator — hides behind a haughty architectural deception.

Ships heavily laden nudge the high lock gates and slide silently across the Great Float to the inner docks. They edge past floury grain terminals and great steel bridges raised in salute. On their port side a tall dust-clad castellated tower reaches from a carelessly restored engine house. This once-handsome structure was built by Bernard Hartley, son of the brilliant and occasionally whimsical Jesse

---

*one of which was sealed off in 1986.

Hartley's hydraulic tower (completed in the 1860s).
Photograph: Private Collection

Hartley, the leading designer for the port of Liverpool. Completed in 1863 the tower, which at that time possessed a tall spire of open lanterns, provided the hydraulic power for bridges and heavy tracking gates.

Today the comparative activity of the inner wharfs is unmatched by the old docks closer to the river, for much of that area is mean and broken. A lonely red brick pump room is reflected in the motionless waters of Wallasey dock with stark inverted beauty. Until recently a maze of crazy paving and weed-covered railway tracks radiated towards the so-called South Reserve goods yard and converged into the semi-darkness of a palatial and obsolete City South Freight terminus. Skeleton-like buffers averted their bony heads from a dreary boxed-in cattle run that once fed the lairages with goaded cattle from Ireland.

One wonders what will eventually become of the remaining buildings and the spacious waters where solemn anglers and silent tide-stained ferry boats have replaced the restless hubbub of loading, the fascination of controversy, and celebrations the like of which Merseyside will never witness again.

Wallasey Dock, 1984.
Photograph: Alison Groves

One of dockland's abandoned buildings, 1984.
Photograph: Alison Groves

The deserted cattle run.   Photograph: Alison Groves

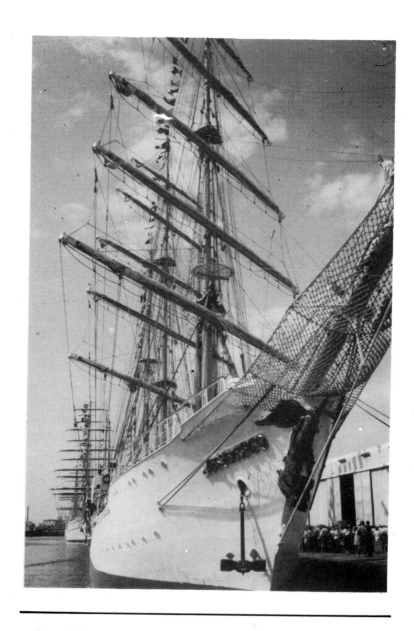

The tall ships come to Birkenhead, 1984 ... a reminder of past glories.

Photographs:
    Maurice Hope

Boats of the Mersey photographed in Birkenhead Docks.
Photographs: Maurice Hope

Photograph: Maurice Hope

By early 1820s Liverpool had grown fat on cotton and slaves. Rumours of glittering fortunes that reached Ireland and pushed far into Lancashire caused thousands of immigrants to flood the city in search of easy prizes. The exploding population demanded houses and — at the expense of a fine plan that had been proposed for the suburbs — shabby terraces soon huddled together in suffocating alleys. Dockside taverns seethed with strange accents and quick tempers and, as stories of poverty and crime multiplied, Liverpool's name became seriously tarnished.

In 1823 the port itself had reached a very serious crisis, for her seven docks were quite incapable of handling the huge volume of cargo swarming up the river from the Americas, the Indies and Africa. Often scores of vessels queued in the Narrows, an easy prey to violent gales, while the quays themselves were congested with ships temporarily immovable in the face of adverse weather conditons. While owners stormed, dockers and crews bickered and brawled, and the city authorities shook their heads and talked unavailingly. The optimism that had greeted the opening of Princes dock in 1821 had evaporated as its inadequacy had become apparent. A radical project for further construction was the only answer, and the authorities' discussions led them to consider the conversion into docks of some of the riverside yards belonging to well-established shipbuilders and repairers. Naturally the shipwrights involved were angered by the prospect of being ejected from their thriving sites and it was against this background that William Laird set off from Liverpool to explore the Cheshire bank of the river.

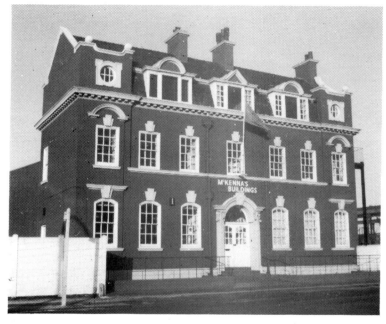

McKenna's buildings. One of the few dockland houses to have survived the ravages of the twnetieth century.   Photograph: Maurice Hope

In the early years of the nineteenth century a few hardy merchants had erected villas near Woodside, and there is no doubt that, despite some little concern regarding pollution of the Seacombe shores of Wallasey Pool, the air was clear and countryside unspoilt. In addition Wirral offered a gentle pace, attractive views and drinking water that tasted like wine.

The Scotsman William Laird had come down to Liverpool in 1810. Having set up an agency for Watt's steam engines, he also specialised in boiler-making and ship repairing. In 1824 Laird directed his attention towards Wallasey Pool, a site he considered ideal for the construction of badly-needed docks, and for the establishment of an iron works. At the incredibly low price of £80 per acre he purchased from Francis Price, the owner of the estate, a large tract of marshy

William Laird.   Photograph: Private Collection

land, set up his factory, and persuaded several of his friends, including Sir John Tobin, a wealthy ship owner, to make similar investments. The new land owners commissioned Alexander Nimmo to draw up plans for the development of the pool. In 1828 Nimmo submitted ideas for a dock system and trans-Wirral canal to his influential colleagues, Thomas Telford and Robert Stephenson. From the brow of Bidston Hill on a breezy afternoon in 1828 an excited Telford exclaimed "Why, they have placed Liverpool on the wrong side of the Mersey!"

Excitement however turned to disenchantment when the cost was estimated at £1½ million. The entire project was in jeopardy. Laird had envisaged an industrial and social adventure. Disturbed by the squalor of Liverpool he had dreamed of a town with full employment and wide open spaces for recreation. It seemed to him that the imaginative transformation of Wallasey Pool, offering as it would, wonderful commercial opportunities, was an essential part of the venture. And yet the sheer magnitude of the task was daunting. The only alternative was to proceed with a second plan, one which deferred considerable portions of the first. Two months later a further report was published and with the cost halved, and determination doubled, the initiators prepared themselves for the commencement of a less spectacular alternative.

At this precise moment a violent flurry of activity swept across the river from a nervously indignant Liverpool Corporation. Having concluded that the Birkenhead episode was 'contary to the interests of the port' the Corporation resolved 'to purchase all the property they could acquire in Wallasey Pool to counteract the plan'. Two wily reprensentatives were selected, one to negotiate with Mr. Laird, the other to contend with Mr. Price. It is likely that the delegates gave an impression that the site would in any event be used for dock construction: at least it was stated that the pool was to be appropriated 'to purposes of trade connected with the Port of Liverpool'. The deception (if it were a deception) worked like magic as both Laird and Price disposed of their holdings for an impressive £726 per acre.

Some little time later the Liverpool Dock Committee assembled and implied that it would not be necessary, after all, to develop the Birkenhead site as 'dock accommodation would be amply sufficient to supply the wants of this port for many years to come'. Tobin and Telford were furious. Telford accused Laird of indulging himself in a 'premeditated and collusive transaction in investment and speculation' and Tobin was so incensed that he immediately sold all of his eighty three acres (undoubtedly at a fabulous profit!).

Though it is not feasible to count the cost of suppressing William Laird's dream of a new city of ships, it is clear that the financial burdens proved too heavy for Liverpool's treasury. Neither did the tactics solve any problems for, despite the construction of several new docks along the Lancashire shores, the volume of river traffic again reached a critical level. In 1840, the year Cunard introduced their first trans-Atlantic passenger service from the Mersey, no fewer than 16,000 craft entered the estuary.

In 1844 Liverpool sold back much of its Wirral lands. Sadly William Laird had by then died. It was however poetically just that his son, John was in a position to purchase those contentious acres and to inaugurate a system of docks which today covers the entire Pool.

And so commenced what the 'Liverpool Mail' called a 'New Era in the commercial Celebration of the Port'. The journal, overjoyed by the effect upon its circulation of an occasion as wonderful as the laying of the foundation stone, anticipated the event with a bold poster proclaiming:

EXTRAORDINARY NOVELTY

. . . the LIVERPOOL MAIL

HAVE ENGAGED AT

ENORMOUS EXPENSE

A number of eminent artists

from the Metropolis

for the express purpose of

doing justice to the

GREAT EVENT by presenting . . .

a SERIES OF VIEWS OF THE

PRINCIPAL SCENES OF THE

FESTIVITIES.

The new Dock Commissioners appointed as their chief engineer James Meadows Rendel, an asset to any committee and a social Prince Charming. His plans comprised a dam across the mouth of the Pool, and a low water basin and dock. On 23rd October 1844, a procession gathered in the streets that William Laird had made for his workers. A parade of 16,000 made its way to the wide sands where 50,000 spectators had already gathered to behold the laying of the stone.

Rendel theatrically buried a bottle containing his plans in a specially prepared furrow and as canons roared and the Dragoons' trumpets flourished, Sir Philip Egerton cemented the great stone with a silver trowel. After a prayer the multitude dispersed to enjoy 'the grand festival', including a dazzling firework display in Argyle Street. Grange Lane Station formed an unexpectedly sumptuous setting for the official banquet at which Mr. Laird himself presided, and, according to a contemporary chronicle 'the pleasure of the merry mingling dance was prolonged until 5.00 a.m., at which hour... the town went to bed to dream of the great future in store for it'.

Three years later, on April 5th, 1847 a small fragment of that great future was realised. Again, streets were bedecked with flags and flowers and, it is said, Woodside ferry boats brought 58,000 passengers across the river to join the celebrations. At last two small

The entrance to Joseph Paxton's magnificent park.
Photograph: Valentine's series

The boat house, Birkenhead Park.
Photograph: Hugo Lang & Co., Liverpool

docks, the Egerton and Morpeth, were to be approved and applauded, a nearby railway link was to be unveiled and Joseph Paxton's magnificent park was to be opened.

From the estuary Viscount Morpeth, M.P., passed through the dock basin aboard John Laird's *Lord Warden*, declared the docks open, and led the ovation as the *Oregon* entered the new basin carrying guano from Patagonia. Again there was much intensive merry-making; dock workers who were given a day's holiday with pay threw their caps high, and fine sentiments were expressed by Sir Philip Egerton and Lord Morpeth who hoped that friendship would prevail between Birkenhead and Liverpool and that one day both towns would unite to form a single great port.

Entertainments in the new park maintained a rural flavour. There was 'a Donkey Race (no carrots allowed), a Grinning Match through Six Horse Collars, and a Foot Race open to All the World'. After the festival the 'Liverpool Mercury' commented: 'Birkenhead is no longer a rural place . . . It is now a Commercial Port on the shores of which, a few years ago, the lonely song of the humble fisherman alone broke the silence which prevailed. Birkenhead commenced business on its own account yesterday'.

The potent chemistry of fitting out and rigging a port stimulated exactly the kind of invasion that had so disturbed the growth of Liverpool a generation earlier. Builders were overpowered by

The opening of Birkenhead Docks, 1847.

A sports festival and firework display were held to celebrate the opening of Birkenhead Docks.

demands for housing for immigrants who crowded into the town to carve out tunnels, to raise dams and to quarry and chisel stone. Conflicting interests of suburb and dock-land increased as splendid houses were encircled by quay walls, gas works and warehouses. With a half-smile the residents of Hamilton Square shuffled uneasily.

But 1847 was an erratic year. The dock scheme of 1844 was far from complete. Instead of an elaborate sea wall across the Pool's mouth there was a temporary embankment. In the summer, matters deteriorated quickly when the Dock Commissioners admitted that funds were exhausted. Before the end of the year work was halted and thousands left the town never to return. Meantime, ship-building at Laird's was almost at a standstill, for although long ago in 1829 the company had floated its first iron-hulled steamer into the Pool, the 'iron policy' had not generally gained acceptance, and orders were scarce. In the town a third of the houses lay empty. 'Grass grew in many of the principal streets — Price Street grew a notable crop of dog daisies and its sole occupants were donkeys grazing, and geese . . .

'Birkenhead . . . was a splendid ruin'.

For the next decade efforts to re-establish a responsible construction policy foundered on the muddy banks of personal and political intrigue. Following a mysterious financial scandal parliamentary assistance was sought, the appointment of the Dock Commissioners repealed, and a board of Trustees established. Rendel, the butt of much criticism, was replaced by James

Abernethy. And yet even when work recommenced the dam was erected 'in a temporary manner'. Rendel was re-appointed together with the highly reputable Thomas Brassey who lived in Whetstone Lane. Labour was imported and the project stuttered forward again. It gathered momentum as Brassey worked feverishly on his dam, yet on March 14th, 1854, within a stone's throw of completion the ill-fated dam burst and collapsed into the river. Brassey, bewildered, offered to restore the structure at his own expense — an impossible task — then he gently wriggled out of the project. In 1855 Birkenhead Docks again passed into the hands of Liverpool Corporation. Liverpool hesitated wearily, Manchester grumbled about lost trade, and finally, in 1857, Parliament passed the Mersey Docks and Harbour Board Act under which management was vested in a single public trust.

At about the same time the churlish issues surrounding shipbuilding were eased. In 1856 Lloyds accepted the risk of iron and, encouraged by new contracts, John Laird, who had dedicated these later years to shipping matters, moved his yard to its present river site as we have seen. Across the years his premises spread and eventually enveloped the waterfront from Woodside to Rock Ferry.

Towards 1860 the oldest docks were rebuilt and Bernard Hartley revised Rendel's plans, many features of which were pronounced

'John Laird's Shipbuilding Yard Mid Nineteenth Century' by A. McLure. Woodside Hotel is on the right.

unsafe. And so as the restless pioneering manners cooled, a programme of dock construction continued, the successful progress of which constituted an obliging anti-climax to such a tempestuous history.

In 1891 when John Masefield arrived at Woodside Station, he marvelled at the sight that greeted him: a river 'full of ships of all sorts; two cities full of ships. In the docks on both sides were masts, sails, flags of ships in fifties and hundreds'.

That at least would have pleased William Laird.

An impression, by John Cobb, of Laird's Shipyard, 1975.

Photograph: Private Collection

Mersey Ferry Boats.
Out in the cold

Photographs: Maurice Hope

Photographs: Maurice Hope

... and 'Mona's Isle'.

The Docks ...

Photographs: Maurice Hope

The Docks ...

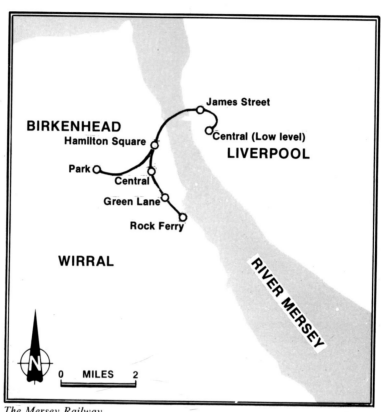

The Mersey Railway.

Chapter 8

PLAYING TRAINS

Just as mountains are meant to be climbed so rivers, and especially, it seems, the Mersey, are there to be crossed. The ubiquitous ferry boat was all very well but it should not be imagined that Victorian speculators were content to leave matters there. Bridges and tunnels loomed large in debates of the day, and it was all but inevitable, particularly in an age of railway mania, that someone should one day suggest a railway line under the river.

Wirral, with her low profile and scattered hamlets, was fair game for the railways speculators many of whom were more than willing to accept the challenge of linking the banks of the Dee with the Mersey shores, or even, in a moment of boldness or madness, the black interior of Liverpool with Wirral's advancing communities.

Perhaps it would not be inappropriate to consider the opening of the under river line in the context of some of the other railway adventures of Wirral.

Popular approval for the main Chester to Birkenhead line had not been easily won. There had been occasions when Stephenson, the appointed engineer, had been forced to make surveys by moonlight: his navvies, crude and uncultured, were 'dreaded by the good and welcomed by the bad'. There were even instances when indignant coach companies had arranged impossible races to confirm their superiority over the 'wheezing, foul-smelling iron horses'. Yet commercial investment was maintained, the line was completed in a blaze of publicity, and the coach companies were silenced.

For the next twenty-five years amazing schemes filled the air although no further developments took place. Indeed two decades before the completion of the Chester-Birkenhead railway a strongly prophetic item had appeared in the press. 'It is in contemplation to form' it stated, 'a ground tunnel under the Mersey, one end of which is to join the intended termination of the Liverpool and Birmingham Railroad Company on the Cheshire side of the river'. Though the idea remained in contemplation for sixty years such a tunnel was finally opened on January 21st, 1886, by Edward, Prince of Wales.

It was, however, during the early 1860s that an application was made, and permission granted, for a railway from 'Seacombe ferry proceeding near the northern side of the Birkenhead Docks, through Poulton Village to Bidston, and thence by way of Moreton, Saughall Massie, Great Meols and Hoose, to the Hoylake terminus adjoining the racecourse'. Accordingly on July 2nd 1866, a section of the line was opened. But the cinder platforms and primitive station buildings hardly matched the dreams, and it was with some surprise that after only eight weeks' operation it could be reported that 'traffic had exceeded all expectations' and 'no less than 30,000 passengers have been conveyed'. This remarkable success encouraged an avalanche of questionable and largely unfulfilled projects including an elaborate tunnel to Bootle Docks, and a line to North Wales across the mouth of the Dee.

Meanwhile the Hoylake railway began to experience the problems of winter. The violent storms of the Mockbeggar coast had been insufficiently considered, and the track was beaten by heavy gales and sometimes buried in biting sands. Special cleaners were employed to scrape and clear the moving parts of engines after each journey. On one occasion a bank of drifting sand derailed a train as it struggled towards its unattainable destination. The engine, snorting and sighing, defied every possible rescue attempt and the 7.15 to Birkenhead suffered the indignity of being drawn by horses. Further, a financial disaster disrupted the company, and as Bradshaw's Manual for 1872 coldly comments 'the undertaking has fallen into bankruptcy . . . and traffic is suspended'.

But the men of the railways, like the men of the canals and of the docks, were not renowned for timidity. They lived in a ruthless age when great deeds were expected and, it seemed, giants grew from the very soil to carry them through. Failure was shrugged aside and crises overridden with a contempt unthinkable by today's pussyfooting standards. When companies crumbled new ones were raised in breathless haste and it was by no means unusual to see under the banner of a brand new sponsor, the same old characters juggling with the same old problems. It was in such circumstances that the apparently doomed Hoylake Railway spread its tentacles to the remote rocks of West Kirby and, from the breezy station at Birkenhead Park (cruelly nicknamed 'pneumonia junction') to the sinning sands of New Brighton.

Frequently, in the '70s and '80s, other companies and individuals continued to complicate the map. Parkgate was pointed east to Ellesmere Port, John Summers pushed an iron-carrying railway from Shotton to Birkenhead Docks, Lever made tracks for Port Sunlight and Bromborough, while a large joint company drove a line through Parkgate to West Kirby — a route now transformed into the Wirral Way, an attractive trail for ramblers and nature lovers.

Yet perhaps the boldest of all railway ventures was the 'subfluvian line' under the Mersey. A Pneumatic Tunnel Railway had already been planned and abandoned when, in 1871, a more orthodox steam system was adopted. During the first few years financial adversities almost suffocated the project, but happily Major Samuel Isaac, a man of boundless determination, but one who claimed no engineering skills, was persuaded by the Mersey Railway Company to accept responsibility for the whole scheme. Work commenced

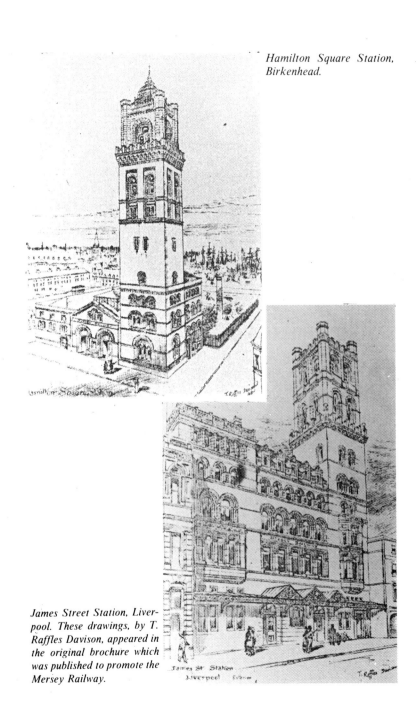

Hamilton Square Station, Birkenhead.

James Street Station, Liverpool. These drawings, by T. Raffles Davison, appeared in the original brochure which was published to promote the Mersey Railway.

with the sinking of exploratory riverside shafts in 1881 and on October 29th, from opposite sides of the river, the Mayors of Birkenhead and Liverpool ceremoniously set in motion the drainage pumps. At a dinner which followed, the assembly toasted not only the Mersey Railway but also the Channel Tunnel!

But what problems the miners encountered, and what miserable conditons they endured! Water, which sometimes swept into the workings at 36,000 gallons a minüte, was a despotic enemy, and even a rock-boring machine which was brought in to reduce seepage and speed progress exacted a savage and ironic penalty. For as it scythed through the stone face it dried the rock dust and increased its density to such an extent that practically all the engineers who operated it later died from silicosis.

But by 1886 spirits were raised and the opening of the Green Lane to James Street line eclipsed even the darkest hours. An early brochure proclaimed a desire to forge links with other Wirral railways and an intention to extend its line to Rock Ferry. Who would have believed that when the Rock Ferry branch finally opened in 1891 the Mersey Railway was almost bankrupt! Steam locomotives had created foul conditions underground, grimy stations discouraged passengers, and the ventilation system designed to clean the air, often disgorged gales of sulphurous fumes. Meanwhile, outside on the bright waters the ferries enjoyed a new vogue. Modern electric trams made excellent connections with the boats, and it was hardly surprising that in view of such sparkling competition railway receipts fell and fell.

Defeat, however, proved to be a potent stimulus, and as the clouds of acrid smoke began to dissolve, another new age began to dawn — the age of electric optimism. In readiness for electrification hundreds of tons of soot were swept from tunnels which were then whitewashed and lit from end to end. Dowdy stations were scrubbed and painted, and brilliant arc-lamps brought a feeling of space and daylight. The first electric train, clean as a whistle, pulled out of Liverpool Central, Birkenhead-bound, on Sunday May 3, 1903 with an under-river fare of one penny, the same as the ferry. But the trains were three times more frequent and three times faster and it was with well-founded confidence that the inaugural brochure announced, 'Don't worry if you miss a train, there's another one behind'. By 1905 the trains caught and overtook the boats.

The overland portion of the line was not electrified until 1938, but the tenuous link between the Wirral and Mersey Railways which had been preserved since 1888, had confirmed its early promise. When in the 1820s the ferries had opened up the villages of the Mersey shores to industrial speculation, the hamlets of Deeside had remained out of reach, out of sight, and barely aware of the nineteenth century. The railways changed all that, but fortunately for the villages of the Dee, development has been of a very different kind, and even today as they gaze towards the Welsh hills they retain a fresh and rural character which the other side of the peninsula has largely forgotten for over a hundred years.

Seacombe

BIRKENHEAD

LIVERPOOL

WIRRAL

RIVER MERSEY

N

0   MILES   2

Chapter 9
CLOSER TO THE SEA

A Wallasey ferry boat approaches Seacombe (1913).
Photograph: Valentine's series

The landing stage at Seacombe Ferry marks the end of the spread of riverside industry that we have followed northwards from the boundary of Eastham woods. From Seacombe to New Brighton there is a long traffic-free promenade with clay cliffs softened by tenacious trees and bushes. Yet between this spot and the dells of Vale Park there are a number of interesting points to attract our attention. Close to the Ferry itself a tall concrete ventilator tower for the recently constructed Wallasey-Liverpool road tunnel represents a new landmark on the Mersey scene, while along the way other and older features are occasionally evident. There is the Home for Aged Mariners (which actually closed in 1977) with its tall clock tower; the sadly derelict buildings of Egremont Ferry; Wallasey Town Hall — especially impressive when seen from the promenade; and, close to New Brighton itself, peeping from above a square fortress, a small village whose livelihood once depended on the retention of underground chambers of deadly gunpowder. Despite a comparatively high density of housing there is a less oppressive atmosphere along this stretch of coast than we have sometimes observed on our journey. Perhaps, closer to the sea, the breezes are fresher and the broadening estuary is freer. One can even stroll along the foreshore, muddy and stony though much of it is, without fear of recrimination. There are patches of shingly sand where children still

The promenade from Egremont, showing Wallasey Town Hall and, on the left the ventilator tower for the second Mersey Road Tunnel.

Photograph: Maurice Hope

sometimes play. And, looking at the river it is possible to imagine it wild and unshackled; to conjure up visions of the smugglers and wreckers who conducted their business from the caves and taverns of this part of Wallasey. Indeed it is still even possible to imagine nature herself as a potential force to be reckoned with along this coast.

To return to Seacombe, it is not entirely surprising to learn that today the area is not what it was. Yet while the riverside charms of Birkenhead were irrevocably destroyed in the 1840s, Seacombe, on the *northern* bank of Wallasey Pool, managed to preserve her attractive qualities for a further half century or more. In 1817 she was commended as 'a place of great resort' and even in 1850 as 'a country village' beyond which were 'stretches of corn and pasture land, lanes and dells'. Pleasant impressions from her childhood days were recorded in 1889 by Hanna Fisher in a poem which ran:

Lanes of Seacombe, green and leafy,
Scenes no more that bless my sight
Where the scent of hawthorne lingered
On the zephyr's wing at night.

Lanes of Seacombe oft I've wandered
Gathering berries black and red
With a simple crown of daisies
Resting on my youthful head.

*(Quoted by Woods & Brown: 'The Rise
& Progress of Wallasey')*

Romantic lines indeed, but Norman Ellison quotes a less flattering regional rhyme in his book 'The Wirral Peninsula':

Wallasey for wreckers
Poulton for trees,
Liscard for honest men
And Seacombe for thieves.

Seacome Ferry Hotel in the later 1970s, immediately prior to its demolition.
Photograph: Maurice Hope

In the early days of the nineteenth century Parry's Seacombe Hotel stood back from the shore near the Ferry. It was much praised. In the 'Pictorial Handbook for the Stranger in Liverpool' of 1843 the following passage appeared: 'At Seacombe there is a capital hotel, with bowling green and accommodation for large or small parties.' The Hotel had made a high reputation amongst 'the gourmands of Liverpool'. Later known as Stokes's Seacombe Hotel the establishment even boasted rustic summer houses and a skittle alley for American bowls.

In common with a number of other river crossings the origins of the ferry itself are obscure although it is noted in archives as early as 1330. Regarding the ensuing 500 years, however, very little is known. Naturally, improvements in facilities were made from time to time and there were occasional shifts in the actual landing places. For many years, for instance, 'a small bay' in the Pool was used for the purposes of embarkation and landing. But it is not until well into the nineteenth century that records become reasonably comprehensive. In 1826 the Ferry was said to be humble though various recent improvements had 'rendered it one of the most useful and agreeable outlets to Liverpool'. In 1838 numerous complaints appeared in ferry documents to the effect that the boats whose main purpose was supposed to transport passengers seemed to spend as much time towing (a profitable side-line) as they did ferrying. Other charges concerned the alleged inadequacy of the so-called 'running out stage' which apparently was incapable of running out a sufficient distance,

The approach to Seacombe Ferry (c.1920).   Photograph: State series

124

with the result that at low tide passengers being carried ashore, or wading through knee high waters, or even balancing upon precarious planks were not uncommon sights. The waiting arms of the fare collector only added insult to injury. Yet there were more favourable comments too. The Liverpool Handbook (again in 1843) commented. 'The ferry is private property and is attached to the hotel; it is very well conducted. The boats are large and fitted with powerful engines, the landing stage is of a peculiar construction being worked by means of a movable steam engine on a railway'. Less than twenty years later the ferry was private property no longer, for in 1861 the rights were acquired by the Wallasey Local Board, an authority who set its mind to improving conditions and tarnished reputations.

Steamers, incidentally, had been introduced by Mr. Parry in 1822. The first such vessel (a wooden paddle boat built by Mottershead and Hayes) was aptly called the *Seacombe*. . It is staggering to discover that 54 years later, in 1876 the Seacombe steamers carried no fewer than 1,750,000 passengers (Seacombe Ferry Improvement Works Report, 1882). Obviously, despite a number of piecemeal modifications over the years, a complete re-examination and extension of facilities and operations became imperative. Although Seacombe Ferry had endeavoured to meet demand, the advent of one and three quarter million customers demanded a revolution in thought. However, progress was slow and it was several years before the elaborate plans of Mr. W. Carson were accepted. His far reaching designs included land reclamation, the building of a 1000 feet sea wall, the provision of new grounds and amenities (including a bowling green) for the Seacombe Hotel, a two section floating stage (to segregate passengers from vehicles and animals) together with a radical notion for driving trains directly on to the boats and off again at Liverpool. Although a boat was built in preparation for this operation (*Sunflower* was launched with railway tracks on deck) the Mersey Docks and Harbour Board decreed that they were unwilling under any circumstances to lay railway lines along the Prince's Stage, and this element of the plan was discarded. Yet a ferry house with turnstiles capable of dealing with 10,000 passengers an hour, together with boiler and engine rooms, hydraulic lifts, and an illuminated clock tower were completed in time for an opening ceremony in 1880 at a cost of £14,508.9s.0d. The next periods of major reconstruction, 1926 and 1933, saw the addition of larger stages, a floating road and, finally, the present ferry terminus building 'in an uneventful simplified classical style' as Pevsner drily comments.

Gazing now at the blank hectares of the Mersey it is impossible to recreate an image of the tumult of days gone by. Cast a mind back in nostalgia if you can and imagine the astonishing army of ferry boats that once enlivened the river and its banks. At first there were rowing

The toll booths at Seacombe Ferry.   Photograph: Maurice Hope

boats, some of them quite elaborate, and long barges with canopies; and then there were sailing craft of every conceivable shape and size with black and white and red and brown sails, trim or torn. There were boats with huge paddles and tall funnels; red, buff, wasp-striped funnels, green-banded black-tipped funnels, bell-mounted and squat funnels, belching smoke as black as ink. And then boats with propellors: single screw, twin screw, quadruple screw. There were fast and slow boats; boats deft, and clumsy unmanageable boats. There were horns and hootings, hissings and clangings, and shouting and cursing. There were fussy boats, serene boats, handsome and hideous boats. There have been boats of oak and boats of iron; luggage boats with circular wooden decks. There have been boats with open spray-swept decks, flying bridges, flush decks, three decks; double enders, mail boats; boats with side-lever engines, patent smoke consumers, feathery floats, timber awnings; boats with glass saloons, luxury candle lit saloons, saloons illuminated by gas from gasometers below deck; boats for towing, for walking round, for dancing and wining and dining on. There have been boats for twenty passengers and boats for two thousand. They have carried businessmen, pleasure seekers, huntsmen in red, smugglers and settlers. They have conveyed cows and sheep, horses and carts, stacks of hay, baskets of fish, and panniers of royal mail. They have shouldered vans and lorries, steam driven wagons and landaulettes.

The Bidston, *1903.*
Photographs: Keith Lewis

The Francis Storey, *1922.*

Mountwood, *1960*.

Some boats have sat on their anchors and have sunk, some have made courageous rescues, some have collided. There have been those who have lived out their post-ferrying lives as dumb barges, as tenders to great liners, as hospital ships, Aegean ferries, war ships; as blockade runners, or landing stages. But since the golden days when the Mersey ferries carried 32,000,000 passengers in a single twelve month period from 1919 to 1920, there have been fewer and fewer boats and fewer landing places.

Only Seacombe and Woodside remain in service now and, at the time of writing, although the Transport Executive maintain three diesel ferry boats (T.S.M.V.s 'Mountwood' and 'Woodchurch', of 1960, and 'Overchurch' of 1962) in addition to the cruise/restaurant ship 'Royal Iris', usually only one of these may be seen at any time ploughing a lonely triangular route between the two Wirral stations and Liverpool Pier Head.

Yet memories of the hustle and bustle are slow to fade. While the river reflects the attenuation of a way of life there are many who can gaze at its emptiness and can re-create scenes of immense activity. Conversations that reach back to the early years of the century are filled with vivid images of, for example,

> 'coasting schooners, may be twenty or thirty anchored up river . . . . . . the truly wonderful sight of seeing them all leaving under various states of sail when the wind was at last favourable . . . . . . the black funnels of the Booth line ships, their names taken from the saints, the red funnels of Cunard, the yellow of White Star, the pink of Bibbys.

128

The sturdy Woodchurch, *1960, in Birkenhead's Morpeth Dock.*
Photograph: Alison Groves

There were ships whose names were taken from trades
and professions, from counties, from Greek mythology . .
. . . Occasionally one would see the big four-master sailing
vessels, the grain racers from Australia, a truly wonderful
sight, some with sails set whilst under tow . . . . .'
Fred Hoblyn

Others remember with special affection the Isle of Man boats —
the *Monas*, the *Snaefells*, the *Ben-my-Chrees' and the Manxmen* — or
the North Wales steamers with their long pale yellow funnels — the
St. Tudnos, St. Trillos and *St. Seiriols*.

As Daisy Tudor sailed over the water from Seacombe to Liverpool
in the early '20s she said, 'You could hardly move for all them boats'.
Such observations made from the decks of the Mersey ferries could
fill volumes.

At the conclusion of their chapter relating to the Mersey services in
'West Coast Steamers' 1966, Duckworth and Langmuir comment
that they represent 'a system of great public value and interest'. The
authors also single out 'the remarkable freedom from serious
accident' for special mention 'Considering the tides and the amount
of shipping so frequently moored and under way in the Mersey this
freedom speakes volumes for the skill of the ships' navigators and the
reliability of the machinery'.

Yet in recent years one crisis has followed another. In June 1977
with the remaining services under threat J.E. Allison argued* that as
the privilege of ferry was granted in 1330 by the Crown 'is not the
right to extinguish it one which still belongs to the Crown and the
Crown only?' Again in 1977 a society called Friends of the Ferries
across the Mersey was formed with support from local M.P.s. In
constant touch with the County Council, the Merseyside Passenger
Transport Executive, and with Westminster itself, they have fought
hard to preserve what is left, and we who love the shabby old Mersey
and her ships should be grateful to them.

Just as it is impossible now to imagine the heyday of the estuary, so
it is difficult to visualize the scene between Seacombe and Egremont,
before the promenade was built. High, drifting sands piled against
the base of the cliffs, and raging tides pounding away at the porous
land or surging and scoring great holes where there were gaps in the
river wall — as there was at Guinea Gap — are Mersey scenes alien to
our experience.

In those days a certain Captain Askew must have seemed a very
grand and remote figure. For it was the habit of this former slave ship

---

*Birkenhead History Society Newsletter, June 1977.

Magazine Promenade looking towards New Brighton.

Photograph: Private Collection

owner to be rowed across the river to and from the Wallasey bank in a twelve oared barge. It was the same John Askew, Harbour Master of Liverpool, whose residence, known as 'Egremont', gave its name to the area between Seacombe and Liscard. Indeed, it was Askew who with the aid of Sir John Tobin (whom we have already met in his role as dockland speculator) purchased certain rights from the Crown and established a steam ferry at Egremont in about 1830. He built (as seems to have been the custom) a large hotel which was popular with Liverpool merchants and their families, particularly during the months when bathing in reasonable temperatures was feasible. (The Hotel, which stood by the ferry, eventually became the Egremont Institute, an assembly room for anyone from the amateur photographer to the political aspirant. It was demolished in 1953).

It would appear that day to day organisation of the ferry was less than efficient under the auspices of Captain Askew. The profits to be made from towing were irresistible to a man of his nature, a situation which tended to displease groups of would-be passengers who were left huddled together on windy slipways for hours at a time! In 1835 amelioration appeared in the form of the Egremont Steam Ferry Company who took over the Hotel and introduced iron steamers. A succession of tenants ran the improved business with some success before the intercession of the Wallasey Local Board in 1861.

A little more than a decade later William Carson built a new iron pier which culminated in a pair of high tripods connected by a rainbow arch. This functional piece of architecture became a familiar feature on the Mersey and served for many years to come.

131

From time to time various additions and modifications to Carson's plans were made. Gridirons were installed for the convenient 'on-site' repair to boats and a large new floating stage was set up and anchored. And yet one critical disadvantage remained — the sheer length of the pier. 'You were already half way to Liverpool before you boarded the ferry boat' they used to say. Yet Egremont was a firm favourite with passengers and with local residents alike. There were highly polished brass fittings, clanging bells, a glass sided waiting area, and at the shore end, there were little shops that sold sweets and hot water for picnics on the sand. There were 3d boat rides and, on the promenade, a public shelter, ever so popular with courting couples, called the Beehive.

It was pleasant and 'homely' around the ferry at Egremont, and it was a great shock when in 1932 a tanker lying in the estuary broke its anchor and rammed the pier. Unperturbed, the authorities rebuilt the structure and re-introduced services. In May, 1941, however, a second ramming, by the coaster, _Newlands,_ caused such havoc that it was necessary to remove the pier and the stage to have them broken up at Tranmere. The stone slip was blown up and Egremont Ferry was left to languish.

Speaking of decay and demolition one must not forget what must be the most romantic cottage of the Wirral shores, Mother Redcap's Tavern. This building once stood just above high water mark (although it has been written that at high tide water actually flowed in the cellars) between Caithness and Lincoln Drive. For centuries

Egremont Ferry in the early 1920s. To the left of the Ferry building is the 'Beehive'. In the centre of the picture is the Egremont Hotel, and to the right is the Institute or Assembly Rooms which was formerly Askew's Hotel.
Photograph: State series. Private Collection

Mother Redcap's has been shrouded in fantasy, and numerous tales of smuggling and wrecking have sprung from its recesses. No doubt the passing of time has enriched the romance of many such stories, and fact and fantasy have mingled in a celebration of the unusual — welcome enough in an area often so starkly prosaic. Yet there is much real evidence too. Several sources refer to a building with three foot walls, five inch studded doors, a sunken cavern secreted below a rudely paved yard, and cellars and secret entrances from a dried up well. There have been detailed accounts of underground passages, (sometimes penetrating the sandstone rocks as far as Red Noses at New Brighton), of pits and cunning trap doors, of a dummy weather vane that warned or beckoned according to its setting, and of seamy apartments peopled by rogues and contrabandists.

As for Mother Redcap herself time has etched in her portrait as a 'comely fresh-coloured Cheshire-spoken woman'* who invariably wore a red hood. She was a great favourite with the sailors and, according to James Stonehouse's report of 1863, she 'enjoyed their entire confidences. She devised hiding places for any number of people (and) the men used to deposit with her their pay and prize monies'. Mother Redcap was said to have enormous sums of money hidden somewhere about the place. . . . 'but where that somewhere was it was never known' continued Mr. Stonehouse. 'It had always been a firm belief with me that some day a rich harvest will be in store for someone'.

The cottage, a strange black and white patterned building with odd extensions and a tile-capped tower, survived in various states of disrepair, and under various owners, until the 1970s.

There was certainly nothing like Mother Redcap's tavern — either visually or poetically — in Wirral. And yet history and make believe hardly constitute redeeming features to the dead pan world of economic policies, and the building was allowed to deteriote to the point of no return. Vacant for a decade vandals were given almost a free hand to destroy the fancies of centuries. In 1973 the authorities cleared the site and granted planning permission for a block of flats. A dozen years later, however, the site had been landscaped: a gentle grassy slope rising from the promenade dominated by a single relic from the fantastic past — a craggy sandstone gateway leading nowhere. As for the hidden treasure there appears to have been no rich harvest for anyone.

---

*Mr. Coventry, a river pilot.

Magazine Village ⭕

BIRKENHEAD

LIVERPOOL

WIRRAL

RIVER MERSEY

N

0   MILES   2

Chapter 10

THE VILLAGE ON MAGAZINE BROW

Rising from the river near Liscard in Wallasey is Magazine village — a community which, before gunpowder had bestowed upon it an air of respectability, was known and denounced as Hell's Brow.

Prior to the eighteenth century the Brow was isolated from all other settlements by a treacherous mere, a wind-swept moor, and by Bidston Moss. For many years sole access to the hamlet was by way of the shore and consequently its insularity, together with its proximity to the estuary, attracted those infamous wreckers and smugglers, who so liberally colour the pages of Wallasey's history. Often posing as simple boatmen and hard-working fishermen they lived in the Brow's squalid muddle of hovels.

And yet the vagaries of passing time have transformed those very hovels into the most delightful and sought after cottages, while the hamlet's early isolation, which necessitated a certain interdependence on the part of its hardened occupants, has been passed to the modern world in the guise of a jealously guarded communal spirit.

The emergence of Magazine Brow as a self-respecting and attractive community dates from 1751, the year in which gunpowder was introduced into the very heart of the village. At that time all sea-going ships were compelled to carry guns in order to defend themselves against the attacks of pirates and of unscrupulous privateers. On entering port the ships' masters were required to discharge all excess gunpowder at some convenient point. In the case of Mersey shipping the powder was unloaded on the dockside at Liverpool and was duly transported for safe-keeping to the city magazine out on the rural edge of the town. But as the city spread towards its rural edges the position of its magazine (on a site now covered by Brownlow Hill) began to cause concern. In addition, the process of carting powder to and from the dockside, and through the bustling streets in ever increasing volumes represented a serious hazard. By 1750 the dangers were so great that a committee was set up to consider alternative measures. Unlike the majority of committees this particular body acted both decisively and with utmost expedition, and selected a more secluded spot on the other bank of the river. The piece of land — measuring just an acre — was duly purchased from its owner, Robert Richardson, for the princely sum of £30-0s-0d. Building commenced immediately and the powder soon flowed into the Liscard chambers.

Needless to say not everyone was happy with this new arrangement. In 'The Charm of Old Wallasey' W.H. Stears relates

Cottages of Magazine Brow.
Photographs: Maurice Hope

that in 1755 'the district becoming more densely populated, a resident in Liscard addressed a letter to the authorities drawing attention to the enormous amount of gunpowder believed to be stored there, and requesting to know what the consequences would be in the event of accidental ignition. The reply, if not satisfactory to the writer, was at least short and to the point: "Dear Sir, It would blow you all to hell!" ' Evidently the principle of diplomacy in official communications was of a later age. Mr. Stears continues 'There was probably very good reason for alarm as the buildings at the time the petition was made, besides being without lightning conductor, were in a very poor state of repair and a great danger on account of the leaky barrels trailing their powder during rough transport to and from the beach.'

However, no explosion ever actually occured on land and the dangers were mitigated by the prosperity that accompanied the visiting masters and owners. Indeed by the 1830s trading and carrying gunpowder had increased to such an extent that Liverpool purchased more land in the village and completely redesigned its stores. By 1838 almost 800 tons of dangerous powder lay beneath Liscard's soil.

Mortimer described the Magazine as follows: 'These extensive Magazines have existed for upwards of a century without the slightest accident. They consist of separate chambers perfectly detached from each other, the intervening space being filled with earth, and the whole enclosed with a strong wall, this is again belted with a thick plantation, and the whole surrounded with a lofty wall, so that all chance of communication is prevented. The internal regulations, which contain all that ingenuity could devise to ensure safety, are strictly enforced, and no admittance, on any pretence, allowed to any except the regular attendants.'

Inevitably, however, anxiety continued to grow and in 1851 Sir George Gray introduced a Bill in Parliament regarding the removal of the Magazines, and shortly afterwards the gunpowder was transferred to the hulks anchored in the river between New Ferry and Eastham.

Meanwhile the little village had more than kept pace with social impositions made upon it and had learned to enjoy its strategic position both as an arsenal and temporary harbour.

Mortimer records the development of the surrounding area during the '40s. Liscard, as we have said, with the exception of 'a few small hovels' had previously been 'nearly a blank' with 'not more than two or three respectable houses in the township', but now 'every quarter affords proof of suburban prosperity. In no place can the triumph of art and industry over the sterility of nature be more apparent than in this neighbourhood . . .' The writer goes on, however, to deliver a timely word of warning against 'the rapid increase of houses of an inferior class; which, unfettered by the restrictions imposed in some adjacent Townships, were springing up in every direction without any regard to regularity, to health, or even comfort'.

Apart from the traffic in gunpowder, the hamlet was associated with the activities of Liverpool in other ways. As early as 1797 it was reported by Moss that many ships had taken to laying at anchor off the Magazines sheltering from the 'westerly winds under the high land, waiting for a fair wind to proceed to sea'. As it was common for a fair wind to take several days to oblige, there were sometimes more than a score of ships sheltering nearby, their crews enjoying a few extra days on dry land. In view of the constant comings and goings of seafaring folk and traders it is surprising that a more sophisticated ferry service did not develop between the Magazines and Liverpool. Unlike Seacombe, Egremont and New Brighton a ferry pier was never constructed and, even more surprisingly, the burden of ferrying was borne — even when steamships sailed the other routes — by uncompetitive sailing boats. (Two steamers were indirectly connected with the ferry, *Hero* and *Paul Pry* both of which made regular calls on their Hoylake trips, but no direct steamer service was ever introduced). As late as 1846 the faithful old sailing vessels were still trailing from the Magazines to Prince's Pier and back.

Fortunately a little more alacrity had been shown in providing for visitors' other needs. Two hotels had been built on the Brow itself. The Pilot Boat Inn, now completely rebuilt, dates from 1847, while the Magazine Hotel, a wonderful lopsided building with half timbering, bears the date 1759. A further hotel, a slightly grander affair than the other two, stood at the bottom of Magazine Lane near the shore. Variously known as the Liscard Hotel, the New Brighton Hotel and the Stanley Arms, it enjoyed a rather more chequered history than its companions.

Indeed in the early 1860s a certain Dr. Poggi converted the building into an educational establishment for Young Gentlemen which he called New Brighton College. Dr. Poggi was a fellow countryman and friend of Garibaldi, the red shirted saviour of Italy. In 1842 Garibaldi had eloped with a beautiful Creole called Anite Ribiero da Silva and had proceeded to produce four children the elder two of which were the boys Menotti and Ricciotti (who incidentally much later in life proved in war to be worthy of their father's adventurous spirit).

Menotti and Ricciotti were among Dr. Poggi's first pupils at New Brighton College and although little is known of their activities in Wallasey — for the Doctor guarded their identities well — it is nevertheless said that they were likeable lads who enjoyed their brief Merseyside education. Brief, for in 1864 the College was seriously damaged by fire and was forced to close. According to Bertram

The gateway to Liscard Battery.   Photographs: Maurice Hope

Magazine Hotel.

Furness in his 'Recollections of Wallasey', 'the pupils were temporarily removed to a house in Victoria Road, opposite . . . the Trocadero. . . . This house was taken by my parents in 1866 and one day, while hunting about in an attic I came across a book (a diary) which announced that it was the book of Menotti Garibaldi. As I knew nothing about Garibaldi I did not place any value on it and do not know what became of it.'

And so to Liscard Battery, the turreted gateway of which may still be seen on Magazine Lane (guarding a row of modern houses that hide incongruously in its shadow). Contrary to many accounts the fortress, which faces the old Magazine watchman's roundhouse, was built several years after the removal of the gunpowder rather than to protect it. Known locally as 'the snake in the grass' this 'masked' battery was devised to work in conjunction with the rather more imposing Fort Perch Rock at the mouth of the river. Rising from a grassy bank that concealed its ranks of guns it soon became obsolete — but not before a local man had purchased the deserted site of Dr. Poggi's College on the opposite corner of the lane. The buyer, who obviously had a keen eye for business, immediately wrote to the War Office suggesting that they might like to purchase the land from him especially as he proposed to erect a house there that 'would effectively prevent the guns of Liscard Battery being trained on any vessel entering the mouth of the Mersey'. The War Office were naturally grateful for his offer but they 'declined to purchase the site adding that if the occasion should arise and the mansion he proposed to build did prevent the use of the Battery they would first blow up his house and the Government would accept all legal responsibility!'

In 1912 the Battery site, emasculated and almost forgotten, was purchased for £1,620 to serve as headquarters for the Liverpool Yacht Club. Today its sole remaining military association is that once a year its walls and turrets form an impressive backdrop for the Armistice services which are conducted beside the Cenotaph on Magazine promenade.

Perhaps the last couple of decades of the nineteenth century represent the village's pleasantest days. Of the Brow's two hostelries Magazine Hotel (which has maintained a village atmosphere up to present times) was then rather superior. It was frequented by top-hatted gentlemen, city clerks and shipping people, many of whom arrived in horse-drawn cabs and were known as 'bay window customers'. The hotel's carefully tended lawns and bowling greens were well patronised while the views from the grounds across open fields with grazing cattle, and over the busy river to the great city beyond, were spectacular. Meanwhile the Pilot Boat catered for the less well-to-do artillery men from the Battery and workmen who were engaged in promenade building. It is said that the Pilot Boat's saloon reeked of thick-twist tobacco, that the floor was covered with sawdust and that the numerous and commodious spittoons were well blessed. There are those who recall that New Brighton's lifeboat used to be based at the Magazines, and that one of the cottages was at that time the lifeboat office where calls were received and the crew members were paid. Regattas were held by the Sandworms and Rocklight Yacht Clubs at the foot of the Brow, and crowds of people turned out in their Sunday best to cheer. On a rather less carefree note other voices hark back to the old 'dead house', a special mortuary which was set up in the village to take care of river suicides and of the victims of drowning that were all too often washed up onto the shore.

The Round House, Magazine Village.   Photograph: Maurice Hope

True, the Magazine's geographical isolation is less well defined these days, but nevertheless there remains a distinct feeling of community on the Brow. Some of the cottages have been in the same families for 200 years or more, and it is not uncommon to hear the old stories related with an almost tangible authenticity. In any event, as one wanders past Vale Park towards the old round house, on the corner of Fort Street, with its squat tower and conical fish-tiled roof, past the handsome Battery gates and the cottages named Laburnum, Eves, Rose and Malindi, and on through the rich green foliage to Magazine Hotel, it soon becomes clear that the village belongs to a different age from the terraced rows of red-brick houses, the noisy main roads and crowded supermarkets that lie, mercifully, just out of sight around the corner.

* * * * * * * *

While we have been picking our way along the coast from Eastham to Wallasey we have not only been looking at history but we have also in a sense been making it. For as well as retelling stories and re-examining relics of the past we have been highlighting various conditions and problems of the present, a present whose attitudes may well constitute interesting research material for future students of history. One wonders what conclusions might one day be reached about the Mersey shores and settlements of the 1980s. Will our investigators see only stagnant imaginations and careless neglect? Will they dismiss our age as a period of social recession characterized by a sense of disillusionment and apathy? Will our capacity to accept the unacceptable be identified as our foremost quality? What will future historians deduce from our new houses and factories, our derelict shipyards, our feats of engineering, our decaying wastelands and our run down churches? How will they compute our sensibility to the environment?

Or will our examiners detect the tiniest seeds of rebirth? Shall we be seen at last to have come to terms with the old industrial revolution and to have begun to embrace the new? Perhaps it will be that our own preoccupation with the past bears fruit not only in a clearer understanding of our heritage but in a gradual improvement of an environment for the future. Maybe after years of unconcern our planners will be seen to have recognised that buildings are for people, the people who must walk in the streets and breathe the air. The modest new riverside promenade at Seacombe — opened in 1986— may be seen as a significant step in the right direction!

Perhaps our students of history will note with some satisfaction that in the 1980s we began to rediscover our forgotten shores.

BIBLIOGRAPHY

Cheshire — *R.N. Dore, Batsford 1977.*
The Wirral Peninsula — *N. Ellison, Hale 1955.*
The History of the Hundred of Wirral — *W.W. Mortimer 1847, Morten 1972.*
The Buildings of England (Cheshire) — *N. Pevsner & E. Hubbard, Penguin 1971.*
The Rise & Progress of Wallasey — *E.C. Woods & P.C. Brown (Wallasey Corporation 1960 2nd ed. 1973).*
Sidelights on Tranmere — *J.E. Allison, Birkenhead History Society 1976.*
Transactions of the Historic Society of Lancashire and Cheshire (The first scheme for docks at Birkenhead and the proposed canal across Wirral) — *Vol. 124, W.R.S. McIntyre 1972.*
The Wirral — *A Brack, Batsford 1980.*
From Priory to Polaris — *S.M. Pinches.*
Birkenhead Priory and the Mersey Ferry State — *R. Stewart Brown 1925.*
The History of Birkenhead — *P. Sulley 1893.*
Mersey Railway — *G.W. Parkin 1965.*
Bygone Birkenhead — *J.R. Kaighin.*
Birkenhead Yesterday and Today — *W.R.S. McIntyre, Philip Son & Nephew 1948.*
Price's Village — *A. Watson, Price's (Bromborough) Ltd. 1966.*
Still the Candle Burns — *Price's Patent Candle Company Ltd. 1947 (reprinted 1972).*
Birkenhead 1877-1974 — *County Borough of Birkenhead 1974.*
Birkenhead Priory and After — *W.F. Bushell 1950.*

Additional sources.

Cammell Lairds Shipbuilders Ltd., Mersey Docks & Harbour Company, Birkenhead Official Handbook, Guide to the Wirral Maritime Museum (H.H.G. Arthur), Eastham Woods Trail (Wirral Borough Council, Department of Leisure Services), The English Illustrated Magazine (1901), Hamilton Advertiser (1938), Port Sunlight News, Progress (Unilever Magazine), Chambers Edinburgh Journal (1845), The Illustrated London News (1847), Liverpool Mail, Birkenhead History Society Newsletters, Friends of the Ferries across the Mersey Newsletters, Manchester Evening News, Birkenhead and Wallasey News, Liverpool Daily Post and Echo, Manchester Commercial Guardian 1931, etc.